Week 1
Beginnings

Beginnings. I hate them. I hate that horrid, "clunky" feel of the first session—that first 20 minutes where course attendees aren't really sure why you're there, why they're there, or who anybody else is. And you feel exactly the same—that first introductory session where people are a little too polite, laugh too readily.

So what can you do? I guess once you've been training for a while, you'll develop your own style and range of techniques to break the ice. However, I'm not sure I'm in total agreement with the common consensus that encourages trainers to "get participants talking as quickly as possible."

The traditional approach has tended to be along the lines of conducting a brief introduction, explaining how the course will be run, then throwing it out to the participants to introduce themselves in pairs. This is OK. People get the chance to talk with one other person and maybe share some concerns about their nervousness, etc. Yet I'm not totally convinced this is the most effective way to start courses in all cases.

Let's think about what we want. Of course, this will vary depending on the training event, makeup of the group, etc., but I think it would be better if we, as trainers, thought a bit more carefully about this aspect. The tendency is to fall into this comfort zone of doing what we've always done and not worrying too much about it. So what exactly do we want? We want people to feel comfortable, receptive, able to voice any concerns, and we want to cover part of the material. The temptation in concentrating solely on making people comfortable is that you can often spend the entire first morning ensuring this happens, and you've wasted a large

chunk of training time. Also, if the course participants are
fairly experienced training attendees, this could just annoy
them, and if they're virgin attendees, it could scare the living
daylights out of them.

Suggestions could be along the lines of event-related
introductions such as "What specifically do you want to
take away from this event?" and a discussion around that.
Or, if the aims and objectives are clearly defined, a brief
introduction from participants after the opening session
could serve as an opener. The benefits of this would be that
people have time to relax into the training. They have the
opportunity to see how the trainer works and to meet other
course members—they get a "feel" for the environment.

I'm not suggesting, at all, that "traditional" introductions
are not valuable—of course they are, especially if they are
well thought out, relevant, and carried out with the right
balance of humor and focus. They will set the tone for the
next few days.

Some of the more challenging opening activities work
well, as long as there is time to process them properly. On
a course dealing with counseling skills that I conducted, for
example, the first exercise was a potentially difficult one that
required participants to work in pairs, and each had to guess
certain characteristics of the others (favorite holiday, type
of music they liked, their age, etc.) based solely on first
impressions. This worked extremely well and was a source
of material for the remainder of the course. It capitalized on
the opportunity at the start of an event when people may not
know each other too well and have to rely on first impressions.

We should consider how we start each course carefully
and not just fall into the habit of going around the room asking participants for their names, where they work, how long
they've worked for their organization, and what they would
do if they won the lottery. We need to be more creative.

Week 2
SMART Evaluation

It's the New Year and the traditional time of year when we get to make resolutions. So what'll it be this year—same as last: be more patient, try not to take things personally, write up teaching notes, take evaluation more seriously?

Maybe I should break this cycle of resolve—plan—think—don't do—feel guilty—resolve—plan—think—don't do . . . by using SMART objectives. I guess people are as familiar with Specific Measurable Achievable Realistic and Time-bound objectives as they are with other training clichés [there's no "I" in TEAM, assumptions make an ASS out of U and ME (insert your favorite here)]. I have always found these objectives hideous. There was a stage a few years ago when someone announced there would be SMARTER objectives. The "E" was for exciting. I never even heard what "R" stood for as I was rolling about on the floor imagining selling exciting objectives to some of my people.

So what could some real SMART objectives be for me in my professional life this year?

1. *By the end of the year to get six managers to demonstrate some form of respect for their staff.* Sounds OK, by struggling on the Measurable and Realistic aspects though.

2. *To have 28 people less stressed as they go through serious organizational change that could result in their losing their jobs, mortgage, and self-esteem.* The situation is realistic, but how can you put a measure on the number of people you could influence? Tricky.

You see my problem?

I've been waiting all my training career (approximately 15 years) to hear cohesive and succinct argument explaining how to evaluate stress, change management, relationships, assertiveness, etc.

I can sign up to 150 days of training per year as a measure, but as a measure of what? It measures the fact that I'm somewhere I said I'd be doing something I'm paid to do, but how effectively am I doing it? Am I more effective—do I have greater impact (current buzzword where I work, superseding ROI)—if I'm training 30 staff or 3?

Am I more effective doing 150 days of training or 30? There's a pretty strong argument to prepare effectively for 30 days of training I guess—the attendees would get a quality, well-prepared, up-to-the-minute, researched product—or so the theory goes.

An old math teacher of mine explained to me that it is impossible to measure anything effectively. He explained that whatever unit you use to measure, your result will be inaccurate by that unit. For example, if you are measuring the distance from Liverpool to Cardiff, it's about 200 miles. If you measure it accurately on a map, it could be 203 miles. However, this is only an estimate. It could be anywhere between 202.5 miles and 203.5 miles. It will be wrong. If you measured it as accurately as possible to the inch, you would still be guessing to within 0.5 inch either way. Again you'd be wrong.

Anyway didn't someone once write, "If you can measure something, then it's obviously not worth measuring."

Week 3
Icebreakers—The Home Leg

Edited highlights of in-house training courses flash through my mind. A person who stood up and said, "I'm here, and I don't want to be, and I'm not saying another word all week," stands out. So does the person who said, "I'm Reginald, and I think it's important that I tell you I'm gay and have just split up with my husband," at which point someone else leapt up and announced, "I'm a transsexual." The question they were asked was what do you think you can bring to the course this week?

Any question can produce equally bizarre results. Even if you leave it as open as what are your hopes for the week? you will get "To survive," "To meet new friends," "To finish early on Friday," and "To learn something useful, for a change." One memorable course that brought a great deal of precourse baggage with it (I think that's the politically correct term) had an ex-couple in the same group. In a course survey under "hopes," one of the exes wrote, "To get laid," and under "fears," "but not by you." It promised to be an interesting week.

A few years back, I attended a course in Berlin where we were encouraged to explore our "authentic" feelings. Armed with this, I tried an exercise on breaking down barriers and removing preconceptions in one of my off-site courses. I paired people off with others they didn't know. They then had to guess certain characteristics about their partner and discuss their preconceptions, e.g., What type of car would their partner drive if money was no object? Which astrological sign did they think their partner was? They speculate and discuss their answer. The theory behind this is that they

5

have made this choice based on something. Invariably this is based on something in the other person's looks or manner that triggers some connection with someone they already know. They check this out, have a good laugh, and realize that this person is different. As a group, we have a good laugh at some of the best stories and because at this point we're bonding, and I can say things like "Well that's the toughest exercise over. The rest of the week is downhill from here." The first three events worked like a dream. People absolutely loved it, and as the week unfolded, they began to realize how they carry perceptions around with them and can form prejudices based on nothing at all, apart from someone reminding them of someone else.

Event four—I notice some tears, some storming out, and some slamming doors. Perceptive as I am, I realize this isn't a good sign. I had introduced a few new questions: "How old do you think the other person is?" and "What newspaper do you think they read?"

Ten minutes later everyone is back and we talk. The upset woman is back and I ask her how it went. "Not bad," she says. I wait. "I didn't mind that he thought I was forty-six when I'm only forty-one, but to say he thinks I read the fucking *Daily Mail* takes the biscuit." How we laughed.

This exercise was based on an experience a fellow trainer had in Berlin where a woman glared at him for the whole two weeks of the training. This trainer is a big guy and can look very intimidating. He's Welsh and hairy. The woman was small and Hungarian. She looked petrified of everything. Every time he said anything, the woman would look at him with what he read as pure evil. After 13 days of this, he had had enough. At the last-night party, he decided to speak to her. He saw her alone in a corner of the room and strode over to her. She gave him that look that was really getting to him by now.

"Look, I don't know what I've done to upset you or whether you hate Welsh people, but I've just had enough of you giving me the evil eye every day. If you don't like me, just tell me!"

She looked at her feet. "I do like you. It's just that you remind me of my ex-husband who used to beat me and once nearly killed me with a knife."

She showed him the scar.

"Oh."

Week 4
Icebreakers—The Away Leg

Kharkov—9:00—day one—Strategic Management and People Management for 14 Ukrainian senior statisticians. They're here for a week. They stumble in. You can feel their eyes glazing over already. The first translated question I get is what time is coffee?

"OK—welcome to five days of Strategic Management and People Management Skills." You can almost feel the life being sucked out of them. I battle on "My name's Byron Kalies, and I live in England. But I'm not English—I'm Welsh and proud of it"—pause while translator does his work. "Has anyone heard of Wales?" Silence. "This week will be hard work, but we intend to have fun." As the word "fun" was translated, you could hear the groan. They've obviously been on fun courses before. So had I, and I knew how they felt.

I decided to get off quickly and introduced my "training partner" Rob. There was a sharp intake of breath and some snickering from participants—three days later I found out the translation implied we were lovers. This misunderstanding was further enhanced when Rob refused to use anything but a blue marker pen—he's an Everton fan. In the Ukraine, "blue" is a slang expression for gay.

"Let's split into pairs and introduce each other. Here's a list of questions that will help you find out some more information about the other: name, where you work, greatest success, what you do in ten words or less" (a futile attempt to stop this exercise from taking the entire first day). I've stopped asking, "What would you do if you won the lottery?"

Flashback to Lesotho—14 statisticians from the Lesotho Bureau of Statistics—eager to learn. I'd been staying at the

9

nicest hotel in Lesotho—the *Maseru Sun*—and had been watching the South African version of "Who Wants to Be a Millionaire?" I thought I'd introduce a topical question.

What I didn't comprehend, however, was that only two of these senior managers could afford TV and the average monthly salary of the group was approximately £30.

So my question *what would you do if you won the 1,000,000 Rand?* had an interesting effect.

One woman started crying and ran out of the room. Another woman held her head in her hands and started rocking back and forth, praying. One bloke got very angry and started screaming.

We discussed the results:

I started first—I'd give up work, buy a new house, spend my days playing golf, etc.

They looked at me in a strange way.

I asked the youngest manager what he would do. Very intensely he described how he would use the money to set up a community where the women wouldn't need to walk three hours a day to get water and the children would have lots to eat. There would be a fund for handicapped children, and the old would be looked after in their twilight years.

"Fine—wish I'd thought of that" my body language said.

An older man started quietly—"I'd buy two more chickens" he said "and give the rest of the money away."

As we heard from the entire group, the stories took on a similar altruistic tone. The crying woman came back and I asked her what she would do. She ran out again screaming, "I'm a Christian! I'm a Christian!"

The final man—obviously the group leader—stood up. Everyone went quiet. "I would reject it. I've been thinking it through. I'd buy a nice house. But then I'd have to build a big fence around it. Employ some guards with dogs—they would be happy at first but would then be out to get my money. So,

I'd need to buy a gun and keep my money with me at all times. I wouldn't be able to walk down the street anymore. So I'd refuse to take the money."

By now a feeling of misery and despair was settling over the course—day one, ten o'clock—only another four days and eight hours left to go.

Back to Kharkov—the by now familiar round of Eastern European political posturing People Management training goes on. I continue, "My greatest success was producing last year's Agricultural Census." There was another sharp intake of breath from other participants. "As you know, the technology let us down." The man on my right (head of Computing) started to go purple. "But I did it and it was a great success." Sits down. Glances at name of the course on his notebook. Stands up quickly. "I mean my team produced a great success."

In truth, it makes no difference at all what you ask—the idea is to get participants talking and get them used to you. Let them realize that you can be stupid and make mistakes—often a critical aspect in some countries. So make a fool of yourself—they'll feel better. Ask who they'd like to have a one-to-one with, even though you know there will be the occasional tears as someone says "My real father"—so what! Whatever you do will be wrong. There are a dozen or so grown up people sitting around like schoolchildren—they don't know the rules yet—so show them. Show them it's OK to get your training partner's name wrong. Embarrass them by making them pair the name of their first pet with their mother's maiden name to get their porn star name. Whatever. By the end of the week, they'll be either crying because they hate to leave or sneaking off before breakfast because they detest everyone in the group. It's the first chance of the week you get to do something wrong and be proud of it. Enjoy!

Week 5
"Go on then. Motivate me!"

I've been in situations where I've had to teach people who don't really want to be there. It's not nice, but hey, it's not that bad. Usually it works out that they're really busy back in the "real world." Either that or they have some fear of training courses, which in turn can lead to some interesting discussions. Inevitably these conversations lead back to previous training courses where they felt intimidated/ignored/bored/embarrassed or all four. We talk at coffee break, at lunch, at dinner, and often way into the evening, and they start opening up about their concerns. Eventually they go away realizing it wasn't as bad as they thought it would be—or at least that's what they tell me.

However, these situations are child's play compared to courses where the people *really* don't want to be there. Unsurprisingly it usually rears its head on an off-site course. You're trapped with these people for a week. You can't easily send them away—they're there so you do what you can. "So what do you hope you'll get out of the next five days?" I ask. "Plenty of sleep and decent food," comes the reply. You get the idea.

Ninety-nine times out of a hundred, this happens with mandatory courses.

Why on earth would anyone think that making courses mandatory is help to anyone? You're off to a bad start already aren't you? You've already set up a reactant—something for them to fight against. Reactants occur when you limit someone's freedom—in this case, the participants' ability to choose whether to attend or not. By denying them the choice, you're virtually guaranteeing unhappiness—for all parties.

There was an experiment carried out where volunteers were questioned and it was discovered that they had no strong preference about two different brands of chocolate. A chocolate vending machine was set up with only one of those brand available. Most of the volunteers were willing to walk quite a distance to find the other brand. Why? Because their choice had been limited, and they reacted.

So tell me again why anyone would make people attend a week-long training course?

Anyway, these compulsory events are usually difficult to begin with, but tend to improve as time goes on. The skills are patience, listening, not blaming, and then a bit more patience. Unfortunately, every now and then a situation comes along that doesn't fit neatly into the "I behave skillfully and things will work out fine" category.

I had heard there were layoffs happening at the organization I was working with. What I didn't realize was that the 12 people attending the course were waiting to leave in a few weeks and were sent to the course to basically get out of the office. This rapidly became apparent as I looked around the room and saw them. They were looking at me as cowboys used to look at a stranger walking through the doors of a saloon in the old West. The chattering stopped and there was a deathly silence. They folded their arms. I talked some gibberish about the aims of the course and how motivational it could be. One of them stood up and said: "I'm fifty-three years old. The only life I've known is this office. All my friends are leaving. I'll probably never work again around here. My wife has taken the kids and gone back to her mother. I'm drinking two bottles of wine a night. Go on—motivate me."

How we laughed . . .

Week 6
Highs and Lows
from Eastern Europe

It's November—it's cold and it's snowing. It's the Ukraine.
I've just spent five days training in a sanatorium in Khmelnik,
West Ukraine (further west than Moscow). I haven't slept
properly for days—(it got noisy at night in the sanatorium).
I haven't talked to my family for seven days—the sanatorium
didn't do telephones.

I hiked to the nearby "town" of Khmelnik to try to
find a telephone. I walked up and down the main street
for 90 seconds. I went into *the* shop—no sign of a telephone,
but they did point me to the building next door. It was a post
office. I made a big mistake—I saw a drawing of a telephone
in the window and began to feel optimistic.

I disturbed a 60-year-old woman behind the counter
talking to someone on the phone: "Do you speak English?"
I asked—as slowly as possible.

"Angleeskee? London? Niet!"

"OK. Can I use a telephone?"—I pointed to three or
four public telephones and made the International gesture
of the tourist who hasn't got a mobile phone—a clenched
fist pressed to my ear.

"Da" and she carried on talking to someone on the other
end of the phone.

I looked at the phones—nowhere to put any money—
no idea how it worked. I looked over at the woman. She
shrugged and carried on talking. I walked out—defeated.

* * * * *

I haven't drunk coffee for a week—I did ask if I could have coffee instead of the tea or the stewed fruit juice—I was met with a stare and a translated "maybe later"—later never arrived. I've been living on the Vegetarian Trainer's International Meal—beer and salted peanuts.

* * * * *

I'm on the overnight train from Kiev to Kharkov. "They always arrive on time," the Ukrainians proudly boast. I now know why. It's a 300-mile journey and takes 8 hours. I could walk faster. I'm in "first class" accommodation (which means there are only two of us in this room the size of a medium coffin that passes for a carriage). I desperately need to go to the restroom, but I've seen the restroom and I'd rather not see it again. Rob, my fellow trainer, is snoring—loudly. I hear my five-year-old daughter's voice: "So Daddy, tell me again why you wanted to be a trainer."

* * * * *

Would I do it again? Like a shot.

Week 7
The Delights of English Hotels

I hate staying in hotels. There was a time when I thought it was the best thing ever. Go away for a few days, see another part of the world, eat properly, meet new and interesting people, experience constant room service. This all seemed so civilized and sensible once upon a time.

The more travel and staying away from home I do, the worse this aspect becomes. Hotels become one and the same—whether they're in Africa, Hungary, Wolverhampton, or Watford, none of them are real. They all have that problem of being someone else's place.

There is, however, one thing worse than staying in hotels—training in hotels. This is fraught with dangers. Here are a few hints and tips and trials and tribulations that I've suffered that I'll pass on to you:

Top tip number one: don't believe anyone. Check everything. Don't let anyone book anything for you. Don't let anyone arrange anything for you unless they've actually suffered when things go wrong themselves. Don't believe anyone when they say "Oh yes that won't be a problem." Do everything yourself. This is based on many bad experiences of projectors not being there, chairs not being there, doors being locked, training room being located next to the elevator, coffee served late, fire alarms going off, etc.

A few months ago, I thought I had finally gotten this sorted out. I was due to run a team-building event in a local hotel in Southport, Lancashire. I knew where it was and had used it before, so there was no need to go there the day before—was there?

I arrived and was told I was in the Barker Suite—a very nice, specially designed training room. I arrived and saw the room setup—not what I'd asked for. There were four huge tables with 16 chairs and a flip chart. I had specifically asked for no tables, 12 chairs in a horseshoe shape, and a flip chart. Ah well, I thought smugly, it's good I'm an hour early—I'll rearrange this, get myself sorted, and still have time to discuss the misunderstanding with the manager before the course starts.

So I set about moving the tables and chairs and muttering amicably to myself, "Nobody told me when I became a trainer that I'd spend half my life lugging flip charts, tables, chairs, and handouts around. I think there should be a training course for trainers on lifting chairs, taking down tables, rewiring electric plugs, finding directions to restrooms in strange hotels. . . ."

Forty-five minutes later it's set up. People start coming in. "Hell they're keen" I think, but I still feel more than a little self-satisfied.

"Funny—I don't recognize any of these people," I casually wonder.

"Excuse me, but this is the Scarborough Suite isn't it?" asks one of the attendees. I looked at the door—Scarborough Suite.

"Oh dear."

I had to explain to two very unhappy trainers what I'd done and sneak away to the immaculately laid out Barker Suite with 12 chairs in a horseshoe shape and a flip chart.

Top tip number two: There are different problems training in London. The main problem is the rooms. They tend to be old, cold, huge hotel dining rooms or ballrooms that someone has decided could be better used as conference facilities. However, the staff are not that keen. It seems a little demeaning to them to use their plush, elegant, Edwardian rooms for something as down market as assertiveness training. There tends to be a group of 10 of you sitting in the middle of 20 acres of a prime central London site, huddled together to keep warm. The "conference facilities" consist of a flip chart, one pen, and a very, very old, very, very loud projector with a screen that was made around the same time as the room was built.

"Could I have more flip-chart paper?" I ask at reception politely.

They look at me as if I'm the lowest of the low and reluctantly fetch me two more sheets. It's obviously beneath them to spend time providing services for training courses.

"We've had royalty here on several occasions," they frequently inform me.

"So. I bet they couldn't get any flip-chart paper either," I wish I'd said.

Top tip number three: The absolute best tip for training at hotels is to get friendly with the staff. Get on first-name terms with the waitresses, night porters, chefs, and housekeeping staff. It will pay dividends in the long run. They know where the bodies are buried.

Meals in hotels can be difficult. Having been a vegetarian for the past 15 years, I've suffered more than most. Again the trick is to get friendly with the staff and recognize the game the chef is playing. Think of it as a game of chess. The menu is just the chef's opening gambit. Counteroffer with what you'd really like, and after some negotiation, you'll reach an agreement. Most hotels realize that trainers and consultants are good for repeat business, so most modern hotels will do everything they can to look after you—as long as they know. So let them know.

Hotel staff really can make or break a training event. They choose your room, they choose your food, they control everything. So be nice to them. This doesn't mean bribing them or giving them excessive tips. It means spending time talking to them when you arrive. It means asking them about their partners, their kids, their cats. Spend some time with them. Trust me—you'll never end up training next to the elevator again.

Week 8
The Okavanga-Kalahari Syndrome

"There's a new change management program starting next week," said the worried voice on the phone, "What can I do?"

"Keep your head down," was my sage advice.

"But this one's serious."

"They all are."

"No—really. This time the HR Department is determined to make it happen. I don't want to change. What can I do?"

"Stay out of the way. It's the Okavanga-Kalahari syndrome."

"Eh?"

"There's a river in Africa that starts in a range of mountains in Namibia known as the Okavanga-Kalahari River. Everyone knows where it starts—it's a huge river. It flows into the Kalahari Desert, but no one really knows where it finishes. It just sort of fades away."

"Ah."

The vast majority of culture change programs go like this: big start with trumpets, fanfare, senior managers wheeled out. The first events are hugely popular and over subscribed. Fast forward six months and ask about it. It just sort of disappeared—no one knew when or whose decision it was. It just faded into the desert—the Okavanga-Kalahari syndrome.

There's a syndrome of change overload creeping into modern business now. Every week there seems to be a new initiative, a new program, a new mission statement. People are getting drained. Any new program needs to be real and well thought out, have tangible benefits, and be fully supported by senior management and all departments. There should be people begging to attend them.

There are a number of factors that will help in the success of any culture program. First is do the math. How much will it cost? How much extra will you get out of it? If you can't get a tangible benefit, then forget it. Your employees certainly won't be bothered unless there's something in it for them as individuals. You certainly shouldn't be bothered unless there's something in it for you as an organization.

Second, people tend to not like change, so if you're not getting any resistance, it's because they've heard of the Okavanga-Kalahari syndrome and are just keeping their heads down waiting for it to go away. You need to encourage resistance—get it out in the open. At least here you'll have a chance to address it. If it's hidden in the shadows, you have no chance.

Third, you must instigate any culture program from the very top and work down. Managers at all levels need to buy in to the program and sell it down the line. This is frequently a very difficult trick to pull off because somewhere in the chain there will invariably be managers who "don't believe in training," as if it's something like Santa Claus or the Tooth Fairy. Talk to them, encourage them, threaten them—whatever works—but you can't ignore them. Staff see that their managers don't attend, or if they do attend they come back and there is absolutely no change in their behavior, and the program loses all credibility. "Why should I bother?" You'll start seeing lots of nonattendees with "too busy to attend" notes from their managers. Leading by example has to start from the top, and top managers need to be rewarded or disciplined immediately. If the credibility of the program goes, you'd just as well forget it and save yourself lots of grief and a fair amount of money and try something else.

Week 9
Change, Death, Reactants, and the Coping Cycle

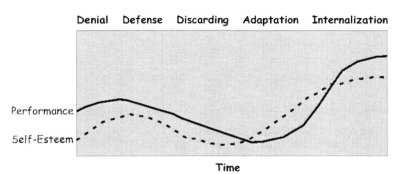

Denial   Defense   Discarding   Adaptation   Internalization

Performance

Self-Esteem

Time

The Coping Cycle (week 9)

I give up. There really seems to be little point. I've just read the article by Alan Deutschman (2005) in *Fast Company*, and it seems to contradict everything I've ever taught.

It would appear that not even if your life is in danger would you actually change your behavior. What hope have any of us trainers when even death doesn't seem to be a big enough motivator for some people?

The article looks at research produced for a worldwide conference on the future. Dr. Edward Miller's research into heart disease showed that people who undergo surgery as a result of this have a choice. If they lead a healthier life-style after surgery they could avoid pain and further surgery and stop the disease before it kills them. However, only 1 in 10 patients changed their lifestyle. It seems that they would prefer to die than change. Having gone through a few stages of the coping cycle (denial—"that can't be right"—and defense—"well I'm sure I would change"), I consciously accepted the evidence and thought about it.

I started to realize that those statistics could well be right. I guess we all know of people who can't/won't change their lifestyles in the face of almost certain death (illustrated by the deaths of George Best, Alex Higgins, and Heath Ledger). Having acknowledged that, I started to think of some of the positives from this—and yes there are a great many positives.

It shows you can't bully people into change with threats—not even the threat of death or long-term illness. For some reason, humans refuse to be told what to do. This links to Jack Brehm's studies on psychological reactance. Put briefly and very simply, it says that as humans, if someone restricts our choice, we will react by doing the opposite. Again there will be hundreds of everyday examples of this. Studies show that if we like two brands of chocolate bar equally (for example, Mars and Kit Kat) and we find only one in a vending machine, we are likely to travel a considerable distance to have the other one. Psychologically, the restriction in our choice (our freedom of choice) forces us to react and rebel against that restriction. No doubt this reaction would be a huge factor for heart patients.

Another factor may be linked to the coping cycle (Adams, Hayes, & Hopson). This model states that in periods of change, people go through five stages—denial, defense, discarding, adaptation, internalization. Each stage is a progression, although it often doesn't feel like that at the time. At the bottom of the adaptation stage (admitting and accepting the change), people are at their lowest—poor self-esteem and performance—but the only way is up from then on. Sometimes people will be stuck in denial or defense and never accept the change.

Patients who receive devastating news may be stuck in the denial phase. It must be incredibly difficult to get past this stage into a more positive, proactive frame of mind.

This got me thinking about how important management training really is. There are successes in change management, and I would hope that they are more than 1 in 10. Perhaps we can change people and get them to behave in ways they hadn't considered before exactly because it's not life or death. Also, it's very difficult to define what success is for trainers. With doctors, I suspect it is a little easier. We get partial successes—someone in the course changes his or her opinion about race or homosexuality as a result of spending time and working with different people. Where would that factor in on an evaluation sheet?

The best result I ever had from a training event happened three years ago. It was after a week-long off-site course. The course involved a lot of discussion and thought by a group of senior statisticians in an organization. At the end of the week, one statistician told me that he had been doing a lot of thinking and had realized how unhappy he was and that he was going to do something about it. A month later, I received a postcard from Egypt—he had left his job and started training to be a "diving with sharks" instructor.

A few months ago I saw him on a training event in London. He had recently returned and was now incredibly happy being a statistician again.

As the Deutschman article goes on to say, there are methods of improving the success rate among heart patients. One main factor seems to be motivating people with the "joy of living" rather than the "fear of death." This was certainly the case for the statistician. Perhaps that could be a better focus for change programs.

One final thought on this: this article did get me thinking about the bigger picture and realizing that sometimes I get trapped into constantly living and breathing training. I know many of my colleagues do as well. Sometimes we take the work too seriously. At the end of the day, though, it is only a training course.

Week 10
So What Do You Really Want My Services For?

A fellow trainer, Dave Hall, asked me a profound question when we worked together once: "What do you do when the person who's paying you to investigate the problem turns out to be the problem?"

Tricky, I thought. Having never been in precisely that position, I had to work through some examples where I had similar problems.

One early consulting job that went a great deal worse than I could have imagined had the customer taking control of the event after being on the receiving end of some particularly harsh feedback she wasn't too thrilled about.

Another occasion provoked a particularly negative reaction from a client when the staff started getting a little too honest for his liking during the agreed-upon "hopes and fears" session.

On both occasions, I learned valuable lessons about contracting carefully at the beginning. Now for every (I really mean *every*) consulting job, there is a contract. This isn't a 14-page tome outlining money, numbered bank accounts, a rider, and standards of behavior. It is a simple contract outlining what I've been asked to do, what the client will do, who's responsible for what, and what I'm expecting to achieve.

I've had reactions of "Do we really need this for a small half-day event?" to "Is that all you've got for a three-month set of programs?" In truth, the contract varies very little. It does, however, spell out precisely what I'm expected to do and not do. It will also prevent the client from taking matters into his or her own hands and changing the agenda just because he or she does not like how things are turning out.

I guess the whole premise behind having a contract is to have a solid set of values. The following values were instilled in me when I began training:

- "Everything we do must be based on the needs of the business."
- "The wisdom is within."

These two almost trite phrases have underpinned how our training is carried out. We tried incredibly hard not to carry out training that's not based on the needs of the organization. This means we didn't run training events because they are fun and popular or will allow the client to get a tick in the box and a pat on the back from his or her boss. They need to actually be achieving something.

We also tried to get the people attending events to work out what they would need for themselves. This doesn't sound too novel except that we tried to use this for all aspects of the process, i.e., we encouraged clients to co-present—work closely with us so that they can run future events themselves.

This isn't as suicidal as it seems. The more clients got involved, the more they wanted to learn and get involved. They seemed to want even more help as time went on.

When I used these values, it wasn't that difficult because the majority of the training was internal. This ingrained approach, however, works extremely well with external training as well.

It has saved me a few sleepless nights because I'm not continuously trying to generate more income from existing clients who, let's face it, suspect you're doing anyway. It has saved a great deal of potential grief and hopefully helped me answer Dave Hall's question by saying it wouldn't make any difference. I'd tell the truth, take the check, and move on. Well, I hope I would anyway.

Week 11
Tension in the Training Room

You can, as a trainer, experience a certain amount of tension. By this I don't mean the tension you feel 20 minutes before a training event; rather, I mean the tension between the values you espouse and the values you actually demonstrate.

Let me explain with an example: I remember many years ago when I was a young, totally principled trainer. I had been brought up with a strong set of working-class, "always do the right thing," "never rat on a mate" beliefs. I was running an exercise that involved a "real play"—a role play that is based on real life where the learner plays him- or herself to re-enact or practice for a difficult situation. This was generally a very successful exercise at the end of a week-long course as people had gained trust and confidence and were by now very open with each other. On this occasion, one of the participants was going through a particularly difficult situation in the workplace—let's call him Rob (since that was his name). Rob felt that his manager wasn't encouraging him. More than that Rob sensed that he didn't have the respect of the manager, and he was becoming more and more disillusioned with work.

We worked through some scenarios where I or others in the group acted as the manager and he offered some strategies. Others in the group gave feedback, suggestions, etc. The advice to Rob was very constructive, but every approach people suggested to Rob had been tried and the manager just wouldn't change his ways. After a fair amount of discussion, I spelled out in typically trainer terms the options—among which as I remember was "If you don't like the situation, you should leave the environment," i.e., resign. Rob was stunned.

I was stunned that he was stunned. "Well if all else fails, the only option would be to resign," I announced cheerfully. I remember feeling pretty confident that I had given him some sensible advice at the time and felt quite pleased with myself.

I wonder if I would be so sure of myself today.

As I become older, I see more dangers and more potential problems in these situations. There seems to be a hundred and one factors to take into consideration. In the training room, we frequently take a black and white view of things—we have to in order to make points. If we had to describe all the aspects that could affect any decision, I doubt we would ever get to the end of a session. Today it seems at times that the only thing I know is that I know nothing. For instance, I would frequently read body language and tell people they were defensive, or aggressive, or hiding something. Ten years later, having spent a number of years completing a psychology course, I realize that I don't know what people are thinking. They may have their arms crossed because they're defensive or afraid, but they could just be cold.

Sometimes we, as trainers, have to sell the company policy—whether it's the latest performance management system, the latest personnel advice on dealing with sick absence, or whatever. Must we believe it? For instance, what if you had to tell people that the benefits system had changed and from now on all sick leave would not be paid by the organization, but would need to come out of the employees' pockets? Then if someone asked what you thought about it, what would you say? Would you tow the party line and say why you thought it would be the most effective way of addressing that particular financial problem? Or would you tell the truth the way you see it and say it was the worse decision the organization had ever made and you didn't agree with it at all? Or, perhaps even worse, would you describe the policy, but make it clear by your tone of voice, body language, and looks to the heavens that you thought it was the most ridiculous decision management had ever made?

I'm sure 12 years ago I would have been advocating "If you don't like the situation, you should leave the environment." Nowadays, I've got to eat. I've got a mortgage. Does this mean I've lost my principles? Or can I pretend I'm "working from within" to change the system.

If you ask any trainer—especially a trainer working in a large organization—do they agree with everything they say, many would say, "Of course not—but I get paid at the end of the month, so I say it."

So where do you draw the line?

(Oh, in case you're wondering, Rob took no notice of my advice and has been promoted at least twice since!)

Week 12
Presentation Skills—
Don't People Just Love 'Em

London, England.

"It wasn't that bad" you say.

He's tripped over the chair, knocked the projector on the floor, and finished a 10-minute presentation in 3 minutes.

"Really?" he beams.

"Really," you say.

"Should we watch the video now?" he asks.

"Let's leave it for a little while, eh?"

This is the first course member out of a group of five. You phoned them last week and asked them to come along prepared to give a 10-minute presentation. One of them has listened to you. One of the others is armed with enough slides for a five-day strategic management course. The others are looking at the floor and giving off the same body vibes you used to give off at school when you had forgotten to do your homework.

Maseru, Lesotho, Southern Africa.

I'm co-presenting. My colleague is winning. They love her. She tells them she wears a long skirt when training to stop people from seeing her knees knocking. They scream with laughter. They're asking questions. They want to have a try. The enthusiasm this group has for learning is incredible. The difference between this session and the last course I ran is staggering.

Barnsley, South Yorkshire, England.

I'm doing all the right things. I'm pretending I'm confident. I reveal some things about myself. I admit to being nervous before I start. I tell them of my worst experience in Poland. I knew the topic inside out. I stood up to speak to 200 civil servants about motivation. I showed the first slide—it's in Polish. I look at my notes—they have, helpfully, been translated into Polish. I suddenly have no idea of anything. I can barely remember my name let alone Abraham Maslow. But I got through it.

"No one died," I say.

They smile, nervously. They're not listening—all they can think about is their own presentation coming up in 10 minutes. It doesn't matter how long you keep telling people that presentations are not the most important part of the course, they won't believe you. Well not at first. Eventually they will.

"Fake it 'till you make it," I say.

Blank looks.

"Pretend you can do something until you wake up one morning and find you really can," I continue. "Really. Trust me—try it—it works."

They trust me—they try it—it works—for some of them.

Back to Maseru.

The first presentation is on implementing the new recruitment system. It's going well. Joseph has a nice, structured approach—"This is how the talk will go: first we'll look at the present system, some of its problems, then the new system. Feel free to ask questions at any time," he says—sounds great.

"The current system. . . ." Dramatic pause. "There is no current system."

I raise my hand, "Excuse me, Joseph, but did you say there was no current system?"

"Correct," he smiled.

"So what happens when there's a vacancy? What happened to the post that came up last month when the administrator left?"

"My cousin took it over."

"Your cousin took it over?"

"Correct," he smiled.

"But how do you know he'll do a good job?"

"He knows I'll kick his arse if he doesn't."

We move on.

Back in Barnsley.

The first presentation is on the effects of the government review on registrars.

The presenter stands up. He's been a proper officer, deputy registrar, and now a chief registrar. He's given his life to the service.

He leans over and whispers to me, "This'll be quick. It won't happen." He then sits down.

"Excuse me," I say, "but it is happening—the first stage has gone through Parliament, and there's a budget of £6,000,000 agreed upon over the next six years to implement it."

He stood up and gives me an "I've seen this sort of thing before" look.

"I've seen this sort of thing before," he said. "We're always having reviews. It won't happen." And he sat down again.

Then he stood up again and in a tone of absolute finality announced: "The best thing to do is keep your head down and wait for it to go away."

Presentations are the most feared part of most "training for trainers" programs, but in many ways, the least important. Yes, it's nice to be able to project your voice to the back of the room. It's great to have exciting slides. It's superb if you can manage the correct eye contact with your audience. However, within a few minutes of the start of the presentation, most of the audience has taken this for granted. The message is far more important. Get that right in your own head and you're winning.

How people deal with questions by the audience is a tremendous indication of where the presenters are in terms of confidence. If the first line in a presentation is "I'll take questions at the end" then the odds are that

a)   they are petrified;

b)   they have no idea what they are talking about; or

c)   they have hours' worth of material, and they'll never reach the end.

It is far better to interact from the start. Find out what the audience knows and doesn't know. Find out why they're there. Find out their particular interests. Get them involved—they'll enjoy it more and so will you. It can be more nerve racking than reading a script, but it is so much more rewarding. But this can only happen if you've got your head straight first.

Preparation is the key. I know it's a cliché, but it's also true. This preparation starts right from the moment it's decided you're the one for the presentation. First, do you agree? If not, get out now—it doesn't get easier the longer you ignore it. It's like that sink full of dirty dishes you allow to pile up. It never gets easier—just a bit worse each day.

Once you've decided, you go for it properly. Do you really want them to know and understand something they didn't know before or do you just want to get to the end of the hour with your credibility intact? If it's the former, then you need to prepare thoroughly. This means that on the day of the presentation, you can throw away your notes, talk, and *listen*. If you just want to impart knowledge, send them an e-mail and save yourself and your audience some grief. Don't waste people's time. They won't thank you no matter how colorful or dazzling the slide show is.

Week 13
Energy Investment

High	Spectators	Players
A T T I T U D E	**Spectators** Look on without getting involved	**Players** Will always try new ways
Low	**Victims** Feel powerless	**Cynics** Negate change

ENERGY   High

The Energy Investment Model (week 13)

I've recently thought of a great reply for the manager who says, "Well, that's all very well, but the problem with our area isn't anything psychological—it's a lack of resources."

This very simple technique can be incredibly helpful when managers are looking for that extra resource they always need. It works because the resource is already there on the team. It's just not being used as it should be—or at all. You will know yourself that there are people in all teams and all organizations who are not as committed to the cause as you are.

These people can be classified as neutral or they could be actively working against the direction the organization wants to go in.

Using this model, you ask managers to look at the energy levels of their team. So how can they use this information?

Well the trick would be to move people into the player's area if possible. This involves a range of tactics, skills, and techniques.

I believe people aren't born cynics or spectators or victims. Over time, they become these types. I contend that people are naturally players, and it's the environment and experiences that make them otherwise. People can and will change from day to day, project to project, and will be happiest when they're in "player" mode.

There are tactics to help this. It can work extremely well pairing a cynic, victim, or spectator with a player. For instance, a colleague was recently involved in a customer care program in which he asked to work with the top three cynics in that work area. The thinking was that if you could get the top cynics involved, the rest would follow. It worked. There was little marketing to do and no need to make the program a requirement. There was a real feeling of "Well if these three are up for it, it's sure to be OK."

Energy Investment—More Detail

On the x axis of the Energy Investment Model is the amount of energy individuals expend talking about and working on the strategic plan.

The y axis looks at the attitude these individuals have toward the change strategy. This ranges from high (extremely positive) to low (extremely negative).

The graph is then split into four sections:

1. Low energy/negative attitude (victims)
2. Low energy/positive attitude (spectators)
3. High energy/positive attitude (players)
4. High energy/negative attitude (cynics)

Victims

These people are life's long sufferers. They are also known as the living dead or walking dead. They roam the corridors of large organizations late at the end of every month when they need to put their hours in. They have little energy and a poor attitude toward strategy or change. In the words of one manager, "They're dead, but they just haven't fallen over yet."

Spectators

These are an interesting breed. They have the right attitude for change but lack the energy to actually do anything about it. They are the cheerleaders for your strategy. "We're right behind you," they say. You turn around and they're gone. They are easy to confuse with players because they say all the right things.

Players

These are the people who make change happen. They are keen, eager, and energetic about change and have the attitude to make a difference. They are enthusiastic, committed, and seemingly eternally optimistic. There are some dangers for these people though. For instance, try this experiment: take your watch off and put it in your pocket. Now take a pen and some paper and draw the watch face. The odds are your drawing is not very similar to your watch. Why would that be? You look at your watch at least 100 times a day—more if you're in meetings. I guess it's too familiar to you. You see it, but you don't take any notice of it. The same thing can happen with players—they tend to get more and more work given to them. Be careful about overusing your players.

Cynics

These are the source of a great deal of additional resource if
you could only tap in to it. These people have a lot of energy.
Unfortunately it seems to be channeled in the wrong direction. Cynics are a very powerful group of people. They
inevitably seem to have a group of people they influence.
Cynics tend to be quite amusing, charismatic, and powerful.
The best definition I've heard of a cynic is "someone who's
given up but not shut up."

Week 14
First Impressions
Are Lasting Impressions

I have a confession to make: I think I've got it wrong. For the past 10 years or so, I've been telling everyone in interviewing courses that you shouldn't decide in the first 20 seconds if the interviewee will get the job or not. I've spouted research that says people decide on the best candidate for a job in the first minute and then spend the rest of the interview confirming their initial analysis—if they feel the candidate is good, they ask easy questions. I've told interviewers that research tells us that if they take an instant dislike to someone on the other hand, they will ask difficult questions and look less favorably on their answers. This effect described as the "halo or horns" effect, has been well studied. In fact there's a whole industry of us out there telling people to beware and stop doing it.

Now I'm not sure if that's completely the right advice.

Recently I've read a fair amount about trusting your instincts, listening to your inner self, etc. This isn't all about hippies and meditation and listening to your inner self—it's scientific as well. I've read of a number of situations where this seems to make total sense. After a transportation disaster, for example, there are always stories about people not going on the plane at the last minute or deciding not to take that train because of some "inner sense." Some of them must be true.

In terms of hiring people, there's an increasing mass of evidence that says that the more instinctive we make our choices, the better. Reading *Blink* by

Malcolm Gladwell (2005), you would believe any other way of choosing would be madness. It seems that when we do make up our minds instantly, we're often far more accurate than when we spend more time analyzing and quantifying.

So what has this to do with interviewing? One suggestion would be to use two-minute interviews. Using this form of "speed interviewing" would seem to be a forward-thinking approach. Just think about it: no paperwork to worry about, no justification needed, no week-long assessment tests, the end of assessment centers, exams, and psychometric tests. Imagine how much time and money that would save!

There is a fundamental problem with this "instant attraction" theory, however: it may not be true. It seems sensible and strikes a chord with us because we've all done it. We've all made an instant decision and found out it was true in the face of all the evidence. However, I wonder how often we've made an instant decision and found it to be wrong? I guess we don't remember those occasions. There is a phrase for this in psychological jargon: "bottom drawer evidence." This concerns the mass of evidence gathered that doesn't fit the theory and is conveniently hidden in the bottom drawer.

So perhaps speed interviewing may not be such a great idea after all. Well, I'm not really sure. After looking at the evidence and writing about it, I've just got a feeling there's something in it.

Week 15
Role Plays and Videotape

If there's one thing guaranteed to get the course off with
a dull thump, it is the sentence "Oh, and yes—we will
be running role plays and yes they will be videotaped."

People have a fear of both aspects, and I seem to have
spent a fair amount of my working life either

a) defending the use of both; or

b) counseling people who have got themselves into such
a state thinking about the problem that it would be
cruel to subject them to the process.

For me, the justification is simple and straightforward
and has been finely tuned throughout the years as a series
of replies to the predictable pattern of questions:

Participant: I hate doing role plays.

Me: And why is that?

Participant: It's so false.

Me: False?

Participant: Yes, it's like this training course. It's nothing
like real life.

Me: So exactly what universe do you think we're
in now then? A virtual world of training?

Participant: Well, you know what I mean. I wouldn't react
in that way back at the office.

Me: Really, why on earth not? You choose your
reactions that skillfully do you? You decide
you'll react unskillfully on a training course,
but of course always behave skillfully back
at the office?

Participant: Well no, but it's different. I hate seeing myself on TV.

Me: So do I. I used to think of myself as a six-foot tall Welsh Adonis with a full head of hair. Having seen myself, I realize I'm not. So I now have the same view of myself as you have, which can only be helpful, don't you think?

Participant: But it's acting.

Me: What's being a manager then? *(although pretending to be far less cynical)*

Having gone through a trillion discussions such as this, the reluctant participants come up with the conclusion: "Well that was the most useful training experience I've ever had. You really can see yourself and learn so much. Oh and by the way, you were right: you do forget all about it after a few minutes. . . ."

Rather than participating in this predictable dialog, I've adopted a different, more pragmatic approach. I call it the no-option, no negotiation approach. It does exactly what you would expect it to do based on the name.

I make it perfectly clear with every bit of precourse literature that goes out that video and role plays will be used. This dramatically reduces the number of defiant discussions, but as we all know, it doesn't completely eradicate them. There is always one:

Participant: I didn't know there would be role plays.

Me: It did state it on the course documentation.

Participant: But I hate being videotaped. It's not real.

Me: Ah well. This is an even greater learning opportunity for you then, isn't it?

Participant: But I don't want to do it.

Me:	OK—well I'll see you around then. I guess you'd be the one on the operating table telling the surgeon he's using the wrong scalpel. *(although far less cynically)*

But seriously though, I do know the psychology. I know the fear. I know it will be uncomfortable, and if there was a better way, I would use it. I don't put people through this for fun. I do it because I feel it's the right thing to do.

I've seen the research, I've seen the results, and I've spent a fair amount of time doing this, so I deserve to be treated like a professional.

Training (like stand-up comedy) is a job most people— especially managers and especially *senior* managers—deep down think they could do better than I can. But they can't. Trust me—this is what I do. Trust me—I'm a trainer.

Week 16
Control

What's the worst job in the world? No, it's not a bookmaker on the *Enterprise* ("Captain, it's a million to one chance, but it just may work"). It's being a manager and a leader.

I've had a number of jobs, and being a manager surely was the worst of them. I remember when I was a young, fairly enthusiastic computer programmer, I was in control. I would stay and finish a program if I really wanted. I felt, however, that my boss had all the power and less stress. I thought that until I got promoted.

In my current life as a trainer, I have a lot of control—I get to do what I want, when I want (within reason), so a spell of managing a bunch of trainers should give me even more control, shouldn't it?

On the contrary, it took me right back to my days of managing programmers. What I'd forgotten is that when you're in charge, you've got to rely on others, and you just don't know what the response will be. It may be that you'll get a better result. You just don't know. You have no control over it. How did that happen in the workplace? Surely as you gain more experience and skill, you get better and have more control, not less. Unfortunately this is not the case.

The bottom line is that managing is a completely different job. As a leader, you have to get people to do the work for you. It's different than doing the work yourself.

There is one sensible rule, though. People like to be trusted. This works for trainers as well. It's not just a soft, fuzzy option. People work better and produce more if they're trusted. It's not easy of course because so far you've led by example. It's probably the reason you've been promoted in the first place. There comes a point in anyone's career progression when they have to be a manager and let others do the work for them. This generally comes when they work out that whatever they do, there are only 24 hours in the day. In fact, you really don't have much choice. There just aren't enough hours for you to do everything or check everything, so take a deep breath and let it go.

This doesn't mean anarchy. This means a sensible discussion about limits and outputs. You agree on the outputs, time frames, and parameters, and from then on, it's a matter of staying away and trusting.

The biggest challenge will come with the first mistake the delegatees make, and you know they will make a first mistake. If you talked about the delegation of the work with your subordinates, you would have said all the right things about "a learning process" and told them to "come and talk to me and we'll discuss it." However, that first mistake will be a big one, at the wrong time, and your subordinates won't come to you until the last possible minute. Now everyone will be looking at how you deal with this.

Take another deep breath and do the right things. One false move here and the next mistake (and there will be a next mistake) will be hidden for longer and be more damaging. In some respects, this is the difference between being a manager and a leader. As Bill O'Brien (former CEO of Hanover Insurance) said, "The problem with managers is that they're always pulling up the radishes to see how they're growing."

Week 17
Looking Good

Recently I've been thinking about clothing—not in the sense of whether to wear it or not, but rather what is considered "appropriate." All the advice ever given talks of wearing the "appropriate" clothing, but what exactly does that mean?

If you've been in this business for any amount of time, you've been through dress trends as often as other training trends. When I started (many years ago), it was easy: you wore a jacket and tie (or the female equivalent) at all times. Then there was the phase where it was more relaxed, looser. If we dressed more casually, it would create a more casual atmosphere and people would be more open to learning. So the tie and jacket disappeared, and it became a little more casual: Ben Sherman chinos and sandals (well not quite that far, although I have seen sandals worn). It felt strange at first—conditioning I guess—yet it soon became comfortable.

As time went on, it felt a little easier to mix and match and choose the appropriate attire for the appropriate session. There were "tie sessions" (interviewing training, consulting with senior managers, strategic programs) and "non-tie" sessions (assertiveness and stress workshops). I don't remember how this divide happened, though. We certainly never talked about it as trainers. It wasn't that we didn't talk about everything else in the world—it was just one of those things that didn't get discussed. There was also a problem with certain courses, for example, customer care training— was that a corporate "tie session" or a relaxed "non-tie session." It was a tricky business.

51

Along with this was the "standing up" or "sitting down" sessions. They often equated to tie sessions and non-tie sessions, but not quite and not all the time. It seemed to be more of an "in the moment" decision.

This issue proved extra difficult when cotraining. Phoning a fellow trainer and asking what he or she would be wearing just wasn't done. It didn't feel right somehow. We would discuss, in depth, everything else—what session we wanted to run, who would do what, how we would handle questioning, how we would give each other feedback, etc.—but asking what another man would be wearing the next day was unthinkable.

One day I was running a communication "non-tie" event and received some comments from a course member in an office I hadn't worked at before. She gave me some really critical feedback for being "too relaxed." It was "not what they would expect someone of my grade to wear." After a little internal defense reaction about people being petty and "can't they see it's for their own good," I considered the situation carefully. This was my first taste of "reverse gradeism" and quite a learning experience for me. I realized my focus was on me rather than on the trainees. I had assumed that people would enjoy the relaxed approach. Why? Because I did.

In my experience, I see a fair amount of trainers' focus turned inward on what's comfortable for the trainer rather than on the audience. Sometimes we go for the easy option. I don't believe it's deliberate or that trainers do it because they are bad people. It's just too easy to get into the mind set. For instance, should we run that session because people like it, it's clever, and they will think we're clever? Or should we run that slightly dull one that doesn't look good at all? Maybe now and again we need to ask the question what are you about—looking good or being effective?

Week 18
Evaluation—The Simple Approach

There's been a great deal written everywhere on training evaluation, value for money, and the attempts to measure the benefit of training. One recent buzzword, or perhaps buzzphrase, is ROI—return on investment. Over the past 10 years or so, I've been coached and coached other trainers to use a different approach. This particular method is very simple and would form the shortest book on evaluation ever written. It consists of just three words: "and so what?"

I try to empty my mind of everything else during and after any training event when evaluation is discussed. The participants need to address this very extremely short question: "and so what?" OK, they may have had a great time, been entertained for five days, been bombarded with the latest theories and examples . . . and so what?

My particular favorite time for this is each morning of a training event. Starting the day reflecting on the previous day serves a number of purposes: it eases people into the day, helps focus them on learning, and encourages them to think about yesterday's learning. Some nice open questions about yesterday's training or anything they've learned provide a good opening, but you need to follow up with the question "and so what?" Maybe you phrase it differently, but the intention is the same: "OK. You've learned that you were a INTP on the Myers-Briggs Type Indicator, so how are you going to use this?" "You say the Tuckman model was very interesting, so how can you use it when you go back to the workplace?" "You say you liked the Egan Shadow Side session" . . ."and so what?"

For me, the hardest part about the whole evaluation process is that the most critical elements of the program just can't be measured. There are occasions in a training room when you've just got to trust that it will be worthwhile. Some of the softer skills and people's attitudes can be extremely difficult if not impossible to measure. For instance, how do you put a value on changing someone with a chauvinistic attitude to showing more respect? You could try to measure it, but most measures are so meaningless that they really don't mean anything. You've just got to trust that instinct—trust that people will be different and happier given more choices.

One of the biggest training successes I had was on a week-long off-site course looking at management skills. One individual was really unhappy coming into the event, and we talked a fair amount throughout the five days. The following Monday I received a phone call saying that he'd been to see his manager and was leaving in three weeks to start a job diving with sharks in Egypt. He was going on a career break. It was something he'd always wanted to do and realized that he was desperately unhappy in work. A year later, he returned from Egypt and, by all accounts, is incredibly happy at work.

I'm not sure there's anyway of calculating the ROI of that training course for him.

Week 19
Feedback

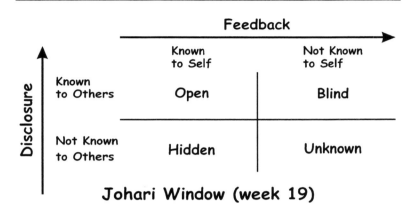

	Feedback	
	Known to Self	Not Known to Self
Known to Others	Open	Blind
Not Known to Others	Hidden	Unknown

Johari Window (week 19)

I guess most trainers are familiar with the Johari Window. One aspect of the model looks at the importance of giving and receiving feedback. It deals with disclosure and becoming more open about yourself and able to tap in to your hidden talents. If you haven't come across this, there are many, many articles available.

As a trainer, this process is extremely valuable—I would argue vital—to your career. A huge aspect of training is being open and vulnerable. You frequently find yourself in a position where you feel all alone and uncomfortable. The more experienced you are and the more self-aware you are, the less difficult it becomes (not easy—it's never easy). However, to do this, you need to be sure of yourself and your abilities. People often feel that once they have learned the "material," they have cracked it. Well, it's a start, but only a start.

The next stage would be the process of delivering the material. For this to happen effectively, you need a coach.

You need someone you can trust. You need someone who is credible to you. You need a person who is honest and skillful enough to tell you truthfully how you are performing in a way that doesn't make you want to jump out the window. This is a difficult role. There is the danger of the coach wanting to show off and tell the coachee everything they should have done and leaving them demoralized. It's natural. They have spent x number of years getting to this point, so there's a feeling that they will unload all their learning on you. Or else they could be so wary of this that they don't say anything useful at all.

The trick is to tread the middle path—give feedback but with love and respect. OK, I know it's a bit of a warm and fuzzy concept, but if you are going to give someone feedback, I believe you have to do it for the right reason. For me, there is only one right reason and that's because you love them and want them to do something differently. You shouldn't give someone feedback to show off, to score points, or to show how superior you are. You do it because you really truly want to help. This really must be your intention. You will do this easily with your partner, your children, your cat. Why? Because you love them and want them to improve.

However, that isn't enough. There are two aspects to this: there's the intention, but also there's the effect. When giving feedback, you need to be sensitive to both. It's not much help after you've destroyed the confidence of a new trainer with accurate but unpalatable feedback to say your intention was to be helpful. It may well have been, but you need to judge how much criticism the new person can usefully accept. For this you need to be sensitive and flexible. This is not to say that you abdicate your responsibility as a coach at all. But, hey, the training life is difficult enough— you don't need someone on your own team giving you a hard time. There are plenty of people "out there" who will do that for you.

Week 20
To Intervene or
Not To Intervene

There's a false perception that nontrainers and new trainers have about being busy and being productive. They're not the same. A lot of people mistake activity for effectiveness. Let me explain.

There's a particular type of trainer who loves talking. Now don't get me wrong, as a trainer you definitely need to talk and often talk a great deal. However, there comes a point where you can only get in the way of the learners' learning. You've done all you can—set the scene, provided the information, created the right environment—now go away. This is the point some trainers have difficulties with. When the best alternative is to do nothing, they tend to think, "So what am I getting paid for?" You're getting paid to stay out of the group. This requires a fair amount of skill, instinct, and discipline.

It's reminiscent of that old joke about a man calling a plumber to fix some noisy pipes. He has a look, has a listen, then goes to his van and brings back a hammer. He gives the pipes a bang with the hammer and the noise stops. He presents his bill for $201. The man questions it, and the plumber itemized the bill: "Wear and tear on the hammer—$1. Knowing where to hit—$200."

It takes a lot of nerve and experience to be willing to say nothing. This, of course, doesn't mean that you're doing nothing—you're still involved, albeit silently. You're still responsible.

A good example is when using the "fishbowl" scenario. This is a technique where one person tells the group of their particular problem then listens silently while the group discusses it. The idea is that the individual gets a new insight into the problem from the others. This usually works extremely well since usually it's difficult to separate wood from trees—especially when you're so close. The dilemma for the trainer is whether to get involved or not. Unless there's a really good reason, my first reaction would be to go with no. You've worked with these people a little while now. Hopefully they trust you and are willing to take part in this exercise, so let them. OK, you may be able to add a little in the way of extra input. On the downside, they'll inevitably be looking to you to confirm and challenge input from the others in the group, and of course, your contributions will carry far more weight than they're entitled to. So let them manage it themselves.

When it comes down to it, it's a matter of what your values are as a trainer. Are you into looking good or getting the job done? As a trainer, there are many, many opportunities to look good. There are innumerable opportunities to come up with the clever answer (because you know what's coming next). There will be situations where you can control people or put them down because you have that power just because of your position standing at the front. But it really shouldn't be about that. It's about getting the job done. The job is for the learners to learn the most effective way they can. The focus is on them—not you. Too often nontrainers and new trainers (and some old trainers for that matter) don't get that and think it's an opportunity to show off.

Of course, you'd never do that would you?

Week 21
Learning Curve

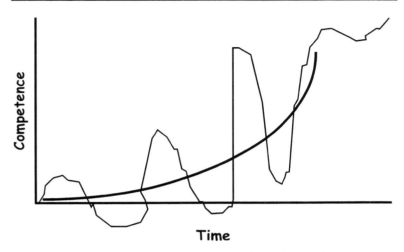

The Learning Curve (week 21)

Ask anyone about "the learning curve," and you'll get a nice, elegant, smooth curve that looks as if all you need to get through that difficult first 10 years of training is time, patience, and some resilience. However, that hasn't been my experience. For me, it's rather like a cross-section of the mountain stages Lance Armstrong was struggling over for the past decade or so. In my experience, each mountain peak gets a little higher, but each has a huge and rapid descent. For me, this equates to my level of confidence and (dare I say it) smugness rapidly followed by an intense "learning experience."

For instance, a few years ago, I'd been helping present a number of half-day consulting events for senior managers looking at the new performance management system due to be rolled out the following month. I ran about nine or ten for fairly large groups (20 to 30 attendees), and they were quite challenging. For years, people had complained about the old system, but now that it was going to change, they were adamant the old way of working was brilliant (but that's a different article). Let's just say I was met with a fair amount of resistance. I got through it, though, and toward the end, I felt I was dealing fairly comfortably with the questioning.

The final session was hastily arranged because there were two people who hadn't been able to attend. "Of course, I'll just schedule these two for this afternoon," I said, thinking— well you know exactly what I was thinking—"easy, easy." Needless to say it was a disaster. I wasn't prepared mentally for this at all and had a miserable few hours. I dare say you've all got your own stories around this theme.

But these are the things you learn more from, in my view. I was at the top of that "Lance Armstrong" mountain, performing well, when suddenly I'm back down again ready for the next ascent. I've learned far more from the disasters than I have from a hundred sessions that went to plan. Now I'm not saying you should deliberately go out of your way to mess up, but it is some crumb of comfort to know immediately after a "developmental" session that you're going to learn a great deal from it.

What really helps with this, though, is having a team of like-minded colleagues to share the pain with. It's often very difficult for new team members to admit to mistakes. Frequently working with new people, I'll ask how it went and get a bland "fine" or "really well." However, when you only hear that, it doesn't quite ring true. There was a time when this used to frustrate me a lot. I have learned over time to be more accepting. For new people, it has to do with self-esteem, confidence, self-awareness, etc. New team members need time, space, and support. I realize it's for me as an old/experienced trainer to give them that and try to create that relationship where they can turn around and tell me,"Guess what just happened to me. I just had the worst day. . . ."

Week 22
"Trainerspeek" or
"Don't You Trainer Me!"

A number of years ago, I came home after a particularly good week-long, off-site management development program. I was fairly new to training: I had only been training for about a year, and the group had really gelled. Myself and my cotrainer (who was also new) worked really hard, and we felt incredibly pleased with ourselves as we drove back. "Finally got the hang of this" I thought to myself as I drove back. (This feeling didn't last long.)

As I arrived home, I was met with a nondelighted partner. She had had a tough week with a stressful time at work, an unruly child, and an "ignorant man who hadn't bothered to call all week," as I was referred to.

I listened to her and did all the right things. I nodded, ah-ahed in all the proper places, looked interested. The mistake I made was that part of my brain was still thinking about a session I had run that morning on communication skills and paraphrasing. I guess most of you are familiar with paraphrasing—it helps the communication process, it shows you're listening, etc., etc., blah, blah.

"So you're worried about your job and wanted to tell me, but I didn't call," I responded as sincerely as I could. Without the swear words: she said, "Don't you trainer me." And started on another 10-minute tirade.

I learned a great deal from this. As a trainer, particularly a new trainer, you do get immersed on the job. Like all jobs, it comes with its own vocabulary, set of internal rules, ways of working, and jokes. It can sometimes be too easy to stay immersed in this training culture and lose a little perspective. This is understandable as we frequently deal with intense situations that can have a considerable effect on others. Without wishing to overplay the importance of this, I believe this living on the edge can occasionally disturb our emotional balance and it can be difficult to step back. As you will know, it can often be incredibly difficult to "switch off" after a difficult day.

For me, this is where I need someone to point this out and bring me back to the real world—"don't trainer me." I can get so wrapped up in work that it can be difficult to realize there is "ordinary life" going on with upset kids, washing machines breaking down, and bills to pay. If you have someone like this, great—if not, I guess it's something to build in to the trainer network and any debriefing sessions after events.

The other aspect of this experience was to draw attention to "trainereze"—that language we can often get into as a trainer. As I say, it's no different from other professionals—doctors, IT experts, etc. Yet I do realize that not everyone appreciates it. Over the past decade, there seems to have been far more awareness of training by managers. Many will have attended a number of training events, and unfortunately a certain percentage will have a negative opinion. I blame this on a certain breed of slick, superficial, incredibly well-groomed (usually) consultants that have infiltrated the business in recent years. We seem to be taking the flak, and there's a history behind so many of the "buzzwords" that we can't use them without someone raising their eyes and smirking in the classroom. We need to realize that these overused phrases like "I can see where you're coming from," "I'll take that on board," "There's no I in team," "Where are you right now?" when used insincerely really turn our "punters" (another one) off, and we need to be incredibly careful with the language. It may seem the most natural thing in the world for us to talk about "learning contracts" and "conditions for satisfaction," but we need to realize it's not the language learners always use. We then have the choice: use different words or explain carefully. Either option requires thought.

Week 23
Advanced Feedback and Steps to Learning

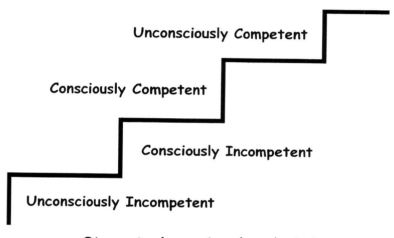

Unconsciously Competent

Consciously Competent

Consciously Incompetent

Unconsciously Incompetent

Steps to Learning (week 23)

Once upon a time I remember being new and quite evangelistic about feedback. It was always the right thing to do—give feedback. "Give feedback without compromise" seemed to be the macho way to do it. It was highly effective—most of the time. But every now and again it didn't feel right. At the time, I put this down to nervousness or an inability to leave my comfort zone to confront people. And yeah yeah, I know it shouldn't be confronting, but it certainly felt like that to me at times.

After a while, giving feedback became fairly comfortable and in terms of the steps to learning model shown above, I was pretty much at the unconsciously competent level.

There did come a time when it went very wrong and I had a particularly difficult situation with a very upset individual. I felt I had fallen from my unconsciously competent perch right back down to unconsciously incompetent. It was all meant to be positive and I was really trying to be helpful, and nothing I said was untrue—from my perception. Yet this person was really upset. Eventually this person was fine, but it made me reconsider why I had become so "aggressive" in giving feedback. I totally believed that I was helping people, and I'm sure I did help a fair number of people with this approach. I believed I was being uncompromising and telling the truth. I realized that I was doing this out of a sense of desperately wanting to help people be better.

What I failed to realize was that I wasn't taking into consideration the effect I was having on the other person and I needed to look more closely at my motives. It doesn't do any good if you're intending to help when all you're doing is making the recipient feel bad, upset, and wrong. As the saying goes "the road to hell is paved with good intentions." Good intentions aren't enough—I needed to be more skillful and far more sensitive.

I also had to dig a little deeper and look at my motives. My motive was to help, but there was a fair amount about me that wanted to look good as well. This was certainly a perception I felt. I had somehow gained the impression that it was considered to be very macho to be as brutally honest as possible. Upon reflection, being frank did seem to be an aspect of training that many trainers went through—and most passed through very quickly. While it would be overplaying it to say giving feedback in an undiplomatic way has done a great deal of harm to training, in general I feel there has been some damage and a number of people put off training as they have heard horror stories of "tough course" and "uncompromising individuals."

As I often say, this is typically borne out of a willingness to help. Frequently, though, I look for the people who help as simply and effectively as possible rather than someone announcing to the world "hey look at me—I'm helping someone!"

Steps to Learning—Brief Description

At the start, if you don't know how to do something— drive a car for example—you are at the unconsciously incompetent level—you're incompetent (you can't do something), but you don't really know you can't do it (you're unconscious of the fact).

Once you start to address the fact, you move up a step to the consciously incompetent level. You still can't drive the car, but now you know you can't. This really is a step up, but it feels anything but. It is uncomfortable. You've gone past the "ignorance is bliss" level and can't go back.

After a while, you learn, progress, and improve, and you can drive the car. However, it's all done by the numbers: Mirror. Signal. Maneuver. It feels stilted. It's how people sometimes feel going back to the office after a training course. They have learned to use listening skills, but it feels awkward and contrived, but they can do it (consciously competent).

Finally, when you've been using the skills for a while, you don't have to think about them. They're automatic to you. It's only when you have to consciously think about what you've done that you realize you're on automatic pilot (consciously competent). This is usually excellent. However, along with this can often come a sense of arrogance, and that is when you're in danger of making a mistake, and you're back at the bottom of the steps again.

Week 24
Small Insights

I was sitting next to a new trainer at a course a little while back. This trainer had only been part of our team for six months or so. Before that, she had worked as a manager. We were attending a training course on "The Implications of Freedom of Information." This was a mandatory event for us to attend, and (like most trainers I know), we had waited until practically the final session to attend (I wonder why that is?). Anyway, I digress. The presenter was a specialist on the Act, and she really knew her stuff on the technicalities and the implications for people, teams, and organizations. She was less adept, however, at the presentation aspects. For instance, the slides were too complex, we had handouts halfway through the talk, which meant people were reading them not listening to her, there didn't seem to be a great deal of thought into the structure, etc. However, it did achieve what it set out to achieve.

At the end of the session, I went up to talk to the presenter. Later I was walking back to the office with the new trainer and discussing the session. This new trainer asked me what I had said to the presenter at the end. I told her that I had thanked her (the presenter) and mentioned one or two things that she had done well. The new trainer was astonished. She thought the course was dire and boring and the presentation was really poor.

"I would have had to tell her how bad it was and what she could do differently," she replied.

I was quite surprised.

Now without wishing to sound like Buddha or presenting this as a "thought for the week," I did reflect a little about this.

Relax: the point of this isn't about "old-fashioned values,"
"youngster's today—no respect," or even "why
aren't I doing a more effective coaching job with my new
staff?" I started thinking about the strange way we learn.
I've seen it a thousand times in a thousand different
circumstances. Once someone masters the first step of
anything, they think that that's it—they've cracked it.

This has happened to me with golf, driving, most aspects
of life, in fact . . . and with course training. The first time I
ran a half-day equal opportunities seminar on my own, I was
convinced I had gotten this training thing sorted out. It took
a lot of good and bad experiences over the next 10 years to
convince me otherwise.

My move into training coincided with my application
to study for a psychology course with the Open University.
Before the course began, I was convinced that I could practically read minds. I used to analyze people's body language.
I would listen to their words, study their nonverbals, watch
their eye movements, listen to the silences, etc. Five years or
so later after completing the course, I knew far less than I had
at the beginning. I know now that folded arms could mean
defensive, pretending to be defensive, disagreement, pretense
at disagreement, nothing, "it's cold in here," or something
else altogether.

So, how does this help in training? I guess it has to do
with awareness and realizing that we all go through this "I
know nothing—I know everything—I know nothing—I know
I know nothing—I know a little bit" cycle. It has taken me a
long time to get this far, and occasionally it works. Frequently
it doesn't, and I'm in the "I would do that better" mode when
watching someone else. Now and again though, as mentioned
right at the beginning, I can see people for what they can do
well, rather than what they can't do.

Maybe I am turning into Buddha?

Week 25
How Honest Are You
As a Trainer?

OK. It seems a bit of a strange question I know, but stay with me: Do you tell the truth at all times? I've been involved in some debate recently with other trainers about feedback and when and when not to give feedback, which made me think. I've also been re-reading Brad Blanton's book *Practicing Radical Honesty* (2000), which definitely makes me think.

He asserts that you must tell the truth, all the truth, at all times, irrespective of anything else, which is quite interesting and slightly too much for me, I'm afraid. It's not that I disagree; rather it's just that I think life is not that serious (perhaps I'm rationalizing) and that people needn't live life this intently at all times. Brad's honesty is aggressive honesty. In answer to a question about finding someone unattractive, Brad recommends you tell them in great detail. Brad sees any withheld communication as lying. This could lead to some interesting training events I guess.

On a nonradical level, how honest are you as a trainer? Those stories and examples you use to illustrate the key messages: are they all 100 percent true? Have they all happened to you *exactly* as you tell them? What do you do as a consultant when you've identified the main cause of the problem is the man who pays your wages? Are you "economical with the truth"? "Tactful"? Do you "forget" to mention certain things? What is truth anyway? If someone asked me the time and my watch had stopped, would I be lying? Technically, yes . . . but. . . .

I remember questioning a former mentor about the honesty of an example he had used. In the discussion, it transpired that there was a lot of truth in it. Several incidents like this had happened, and she had combined them to come up with a clear illustration. Was this lying?

I guess behind this, you need to look at the intention of the trainer. Is the story intended to help or to make the trainer look good? Is it used to manipulate people? However, what would happen if someone knew the "whole truth"? How would they feel? How would the trainer's credibility hold up?

People are a bit like me and you—they aren't stupid. They can spot an outright lie at 20 paces, but some illustrations? I don't know if it hurts if the odd incident is edited to include the key element or is a combination of events. Or perhaps I'm just rationalizing.

Week 26
Devolving Power

There's been a fair amount of debate in recent years about the power of managers and HR. The responsibility seems to be moving away from the center toward the managers. This has been happening at a rapid rate in terms of HRD personnel functions, and now there's pressure to devolve this power further to managers.

Managers have had to make decisions that personnel would have made in the past—conduct disciplinary interviews, decide on conditions of service, recruit, etc. The aspect that concerns us of course is the training role. There is a real fear among many trainers about this aspect: Managers getting involved in training? They'll take our jobs—it's unthinkable!

I tend to adopt a different approach—good! Let them train properly. Let them try it for a few weeks—the knowledge, skills, and attitude thing. Perhaps they'll learn then that to be a good trainer, you need a certain amount of knowledge and skill to do it.

A lot of people these days seem to think, *I've seen trainers, and they stand up and talk and try to keep people awake. Anyone can do that.* Once again, I say, "Good, let them take their best shot. Let's see how they cope when people just want to argue for the sake of arguing or when people just want to be anywhere else than where they are—stuck in a room in the company of strangers."

If you think about it, it's a bit insulting really. People wouldn't walk up to a surgeon saying, "Well I've seen how you do that. I've got a knife and a green set of overalls. I'm sure I'll be able to have a stab at that. Move over." Nor would you see someone walk into a cockpit saying, "I've seen

Airplane twice now—let me have a go." Of course not! It's nonsense. It's just that trainers have one of those jobs that people observe, and because the skills involved are so subtle and almost designed to disguise them, it looks effortless (well, on a good day).

I actually think we need to make it look far more difficult. I think we need to prowl around precourse like weightlifter, pacing and rubbing chalk on our hands, breathing deeply, and occasionally screaming some bizarre word. Instead, what do we do?—sit around drinking coffee talking to shy attendees making them feel comfortable. Well no more.

From now on, I'm going to let all the angst and self-doubt out. I'm going to sob uncontrollably if I have a less-than perfect session. I'm going to employ a sports psychologist to talk to me during coffee breaks and psych me up, get my focus back, and get my "bubbliness" back.

Bubbly my arse.

Week 27
Mandatory Courses

Imagine this problem: You have far too many people signed up for your training events. Every session is over-booked, and you can't get any time off. What on earth can you do?

I know—make them mandatory. That will slow down the sign ups.

So how does that happen? I guess one aspect is linked to the work of Jack Brehm (1966) that looks at reactance theory. This theory states that if you limit someone's choice, they will react by trying to re-establish that choice and responding negatively to the imposed choice. For instance, if you like Mars bars and Kit-Kats equally and if the vending machine has only one type available, what do you do? Research suggests that you would travel a considerable distance to buy the other chocolate bar. This has been illustrated with a number of experiments, and Jack Brehm explains it as you re-establishing your freedom of choice. Similarly, as a parent, if you want your children to eat broccoli, it frequently works if you tell them they can't have broccoli.

It has also become common practice in the sales environment. There are a number of techniques used to force people to choose. For instance, there's the "take away technique" and the "you can't afford it tactic." When a salesperson is trying to sell something, he or she will often meet resistance. This resistance can be overcome by the salesperson saying that the offer is for one day only, or that although the article would be perfect for the buyer, it's doubtful he or she could afford it. These tactics tend to work as they raise the reactance level in people. You know yourself what it's like when people tell you what not to do. Think of *Romeo and Juliet.* Think of

West Side Story. Think of most teen movies. It's about wanting what you can't have. If you've got a teenage child, you'll know this. Someone once told me of a situation with their teenage child. As the boy was walking out the door for an evening out, the parent shouted, "Have a nice time." The reply came back, "Don't tell me what to do," with a slam of the door.

In training terms, if you try to force someone to attend an in-house training course . . . well you can work out the rest. If that doesn't work and they still want to attend, why not threaten to hard charge them. That will really threaten them. In sales terms, it's a variation of the "you can't afford it tactic" plus a little transactional analysis (TA).

In one element of TA terms, there is a theory that if someone adopts a particular state, then this triggers a different state in another. The states in TA are basically defined as parent, adult, and child. So by telling someone they've got to do something, you are adopting a critical parent role, and this could trigger a childlike state in the other. This would tend to make them react as a child would—a lot of feet stamping and saying they won't, they won't, they won't.

Not the ideal start to a course, is it?

Week 28
Cotraining

Running a training event with another trainer or a few other trainers can be quite traumatic. If you don't know them, it can be difficult. If you do know them but don't particularly get along, it can be even worse. There needs to be real understanding and real teamwork when you cotrain. Course attendees can tell very quickly if there are problems, and you can get a situation where a particularly difficult participant can use this. This person may not be evil, but he or she may not be happy for any number of reasons— the prime one being he or she does not want to participate in the course in the first place. If this person sees problems, he or she may end up like my seven-year-old daughter playing one parent against the other. This isn't good, and it isn't professional—plus you can't really send them to their room to think about what they've done.

I was lucky enough to be inducted into the training profession by a number of experienced and sensible trainers. I was taught a number of lessons that Chartered Institute of Personnel Development doesn't teach you, and most of them are centered on teamwork.

Before the training event, you need to talk to your fellow trainer(s). If this is the first time you've worked together, allow a fair amount of time for this. There are a number of agreements you need to have in place. This may seem obvious, but if you don't get this right at the outset, it really can disrupt the course and ultimately your relationship with the other trainer(s). It also helps getting to know the other trainers and their thoughts and values as you work together.

You need to carefully agree not only what you're doing in terms of presenting, but also in terms of feedback and support. Once you've agreed on the split of the sessions, discuss how you'd prefer to work together. Everyone has their own style, and it can take a while to be comfortable with another trainer, but it is a great learning experience. I have worked with trainers who just wanted to run their sessions on their own with no cooperation except when they ask for it. However, most trainers I've worked with I have known well, and they were often willing to run most sessions as truly joint sessions with each of us contributing. Whatever you decide, make it as explicit as possible—it avoids any misunderstanding.

Working with another trainer is a perfect opportunity to get feedback. Again the details of this—When will you give each other feedback? In how much detail? Is there anything in particular that the other wants you to pay attention to?—need to be discussed before the session.

As I mentioned, it's vital that you act as a team. It may be that you don't get along with the other trainer, but it's about both of you being professional and acknowledging this. If you haven't worked with him or her before, it's especially important to discuss how you need to help and support each other. In one cotraining session, it was spelled out to me that it is "us and them"—between the trainers and the course members. This was not meant in a nasty, malicious way, but as trainers, we are a team, and as course members, they are a team.

You need to totally support your fellow trainer. If they're having trouble with a difficult course member, you've got to help out, whatever your feelings. If your cotrainer is struggling with some material or a difficult question, you need to get involved and help. This may give them the time they need to rethink the situation. If you work well as a team, then course members get so much more benefit—they get a number of opinions and different approaches.

Ultimately cotraining is all about relationships and being professional. However, it takes a good deal of preparation to make this happen.

Week 29
Culture

How do you work out the culture of the organization you're working in? What are the telltale signs that indicate it's going to be hard work or fun?

You can spot the signs way before you begin training. Sometimes you can get a "sense" of the organization before you enter the building. Let me explain: I worked with a consultant, Dave Hall, a number of years ago. I had never met him, and we arranged to meet in my office. I met him and asked if he'd like me to tell him about the culture of our organization.

"No need," he said. "I have a pretty good idea already."

I looked suitably surprised.

"There is a lot in your mission, vision, and values booklet about meeting the needs of the customer. However, I've had to spend 10 minutes explaining who I was to the security guards before I was let through the gate. Then I had a half mile walk, in the rain, to the main building. I had to walk past a number of expensive cars—I guess they belong to senior managers—parked very near the front door. I then met more security staff. I was told to wait in a cold room with nothing to read and no coffee. I was told nothing until you turned up. Yes I have some understanding of your culture."

Dave went on to tell me about a meeting he had the previous week with a client. As he approached the parking lot of the client's building, he was met by a security guard. Instead of interrogating him, the guard directed him to the parking area (close to the building). He was met by a personal assistant who apologized that the CEO he was due to spend some time with was running late and asked if he would mind waiting in an office. He was supplied newspapers, magazines, and coffee (milk, no sugar). The personal assistant had called Dave's secretary before his visit and asked her what the registration number of Dave's car was (then informed the security guards), asked her to give a brief description of Dave, and found out how he took his coffee.

Before I visit an organization for the first time, I try to remember Dave's observations and I try to add a few observations of my own. It really does give you an insight into the organization if you keep your eyes open. Look for broken windows, notices out of date, neglected paintwork. This can often give you a feel for the attention to detail in the business.

It is all useful evidence, but it is just a start though. There's no substitute for observing, talking, and listening to people.

I was talking with a lecturer at Henley Management College who believed he could spot delegates from the private or public sector by the way they walked. He maintained that the government delegates sauntered in to the training room with hunched shoulders and an air of despondency. He was over elaborating to make a point, but he did correctly identify 16 of the 20 delegates walking past his window one morning as we watched them making their way to register for a course.

Week 30
Attack Isn't Always the Best Form of Defense

What do you do when you're faced with a room full of people who either don't want to be there or, even worse, really, really do want to be there because they can't wait to give you some direct feedback on the new system that you are there to train them in?

Yes, I'm talking about introducing a new performance management system.

This is a facet of training where experience is vital. If you've been through it all before and know how the people are feeling, you are way ahead. You need a positive attitude, a huge amount of empathy, balance, and a thick skin. You need to realize that you are not the system. People aren't attacking you. Really they're not, so there's no reason to feel depressed. However, I admit the distinction can get a little blurred at 3:30 on a Thursday afternoon when you've run 23 of these sessions and you're still only halfway through the organization.

A digression: I once attended a seminar run by an eminent management guru, Gerry Egan. His first question to a room of senior managers was: "Would you like to save £1 million?"

There were puzzled looks all around.

"At a conservative estimate," he added.

"Of course!"

"Get rid of your performance management system."

"But ours is different. . . ."

"It costs a fortune to maintain. Your staff hate it. It causes more grief than anything else in the organization."

"What can we replace it with?"

"Managers doing their jobs."

Back to performance management: You've worked with these people before, so you know how much they hated the old performance management system—don't lose sight of that. You've had this on change courses, policy courses, and management courses, and now they're getting rid of this system, so it should be good news, right? Ah, not quite.

If you're familiar with the coping cycle model (Adams, Hayes, & Hopson, 1976), which looks at how people cope with change, this is classic "use it as an example on the next course" behavior. If you're not familiar, refer to Week 9 (Change, Death, Reactants, and the Coping Cycle).

When change is imposed on people, we tend to get a little stuck in defense and denial modes. This is all these people are doing. They're resisting change. They're not bad people. Unfortunately, you're the one who has to ease them through the defense and denial stages. It isn't easy, but it's your job.

This is where your positive attitude comes in to play. You need to realize that it's not personal and that these people are vulnerable. You need trust, patience, and genuine empathy.

Don't show the coping cycle as a form of defense, attack, or retaliation. If you are going to use it, use it early to illustrate how the process works. Otherwise, it can be seen as a way of slapping people down with a "I know better than you" attitude.

The top tip, however, is to keep that positive attitude going. This takes great skill and patience.

Week 31
Let's Build a Team

There is a multitude of excellent (and expensive) guides and profiles to analyzing and perfecting teams—Team Management Systems, Belbin, Myers-Briggs, astrology, personal drivers, just to name a few. As a trainer, these can all be extremely useful. For a week-long off-site course, they are perfect for helping people break the ice. People can talk about themselves in general terms—"I'm an introvert. I tend to like. . . ." Then as the week develops, they can look more closely at the definitions and see how they could apply to people back at the workplace. They are very powerful tools. The dangers of course are that people could stereotype themselves or others, "Oh I'm a creator-innovator. I don't do detail, so someone else will have to write this up."

These team-building tools, however, are just that—tools to be used wisely and appropriately to give some indication of how people may behave, not to pigeonhole people. I've seen trainers look at the list of trainees before a course and say, "Ah ha! He's an explorer-promoter; he'll be loud. She's an introvert; she'll be creative." Unfortunately (fortunately), life doesn't work like that.

These tools tend to be written reports on your strengths/weaknesses—things you should do, things you shouldn't do. They're not very good for choosing teams. They are good for a number of other reasons though. For instance, they're excellent as an initial snapshot of where people may be and as the start of a discussion about strengths/weaknesses. In addition, they're great for developing the team and the individual later in the team's development.

A great illustration of this comes from an intensive management development program I ran a few years ago. All week, we looked at a variety of ways to build a team and had everyone profiled: Bill—introvert, analytical, plant, Scorpio rising, creative, hurry-up driver; Jane—implementer, extrovert, Aquarius moon, hurry-up driver, if I could identify with an animal it would be a leopard; etc. Then the final exercise involved splitting into two teams and competing against each other in a management exercise. Three members defined as analysts had a field day—they matched and matched—a creative-introvert for each team, a coordinator in each group, and so on and so on. Finally the teams were announced.

"Any problems?" one of them announced smugly.

A shy voice spoke out: "Uh yes." she said. "I want to be in the same team as my friend."

So the teams were restructured—boys versus girls—and a great success.

Once a team starts working together, these profiles really come into their own, but we'll come back to that. First we need to make a diversion to Australia and look at the work of Bruce Tuckman. His model of the various stages effective teams go through is excellent. Over time, teams move from forming to storming to norming to performing. Forming is the polite stage team members go through when they're getting to know each other—the very polite, "after you with the pastries," "no, after you," "no, after you" stage. The next stage is storming where the team members are more confident and there are disputes over status, roles, etc. This doesn't need to be loud and violent; it could be dark and quiet or sarcastic, but it needs to happen for the team to evolve. Team members have to be able to bounce ideas off each other and disagree with each other. In the norming stage, the team has worked out their roles and can relax, ready for the performing stage where there's a real buzz, high energy, and production.

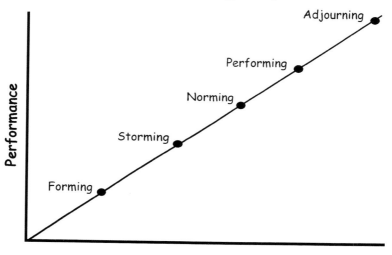

Tuckman
Stages of Group Development (week 31)

You know this is true, don't you? As a new manager, if you walk into a room to meet your new team and there's deathly silence, be afraid, be very afraid. Team rooms should occasionally sound like grade-school classrooms—lively and buzzing (within reason of course) and focused. If you've worked in a team for three months and someone still needs to ask if they can borrow a pen from the pile on your desk, you're in trouble. There should be discussion, disagreements. People should feel some passion about their work. Think Oasis—the best pop band of the nineties that seemed to be forever storming, forming, but still performing.

So how do you deal with (encourage even) the storming? This is where the profiles can come in handy. They almost give the team a license to storm. During team-building sessions, you hear things like, "Well when that happens it really winds me up—that's upholder maintainers for you." It becomes more impersonal. People really do open up even though they hide behind the labels. Now you can do something about it.

In terms of the Team Management Profile devised by Margerison and McCann, I'm a reporter advisor—flexible, beliefs-driven, introvert, and creative. My cotrainer eight years ago, Duncan, was exactly the opposite—structured, analytical, extrovert, and practical. We'd be running a five-day course and really start annoying each other. I knew that on day two at 11:18 if it were his session, we'd be looking at stage two of Maslow's hierarchy of needs. "Get a life," I'd urge (silently)—he was a lot bigger than me. He knew that sometime on day three or four, we'd get around to Adair's Action-Centered Leadership model. "I wish he'd get his act together," Duncan would think, not so silently. Then we were profiled and talked about this. Now we know why we get on each other's nerves occasionally and have a far greater understanding of each other—we recognize we are not the same and see the world differently.

Being profiled can work for your team as well. What may not work, unless you handle it extremely well, is presenting it as a "fun team-building day." Never tell your team they're going to have fun—I can hear people groaning already. They would rather spend a day in a corner doing hard math facts than be dragged along to a fun day away. Make all activities work related—they'll create the fun themselves. People do really prefer it.

If you've recently inherited a team, this day is essential. It will give you great insight into the people you've got. There are hundreds of very simple exercises to help with this. One exercise is to get the team to draw how they see themselves. If they draw themselves (as I've seen twice before) as slaves on a galley ship with their previous manager and other managers as the drum beater, whip handler, and captain, run away. If they draw themselves as flowers and the previous manager as the sun, run away quicker. I'm joking—but you get the point.

Another superb exercise is to get them to agree on the top teams from anywhere. I've seen the top teams as ants, Ferrari Formula One team, 1966 England World Cup football squad, Microsoft, various British Lions rugby teams, surgeons, and Amazon.com. Then look at what makes them so special and emulate that—ants were felt to be totally supportive of all other members of the team, non-blameful, and very focused. That worked. It was fun.

Week 32
The Zeigarnik Effect—
A Force for Good or Evil?

I've recently been looking at something known as the Zeigarnik effect. You may have come across it in advertising, television, or any number of forms, but perhaps not realized it. So what is it all about? you ask.

I'll tell you in a minute, but first, some background. The person this was named after was Bluma Zeigarnik, born in Russia, now Lithuania, in 1900. The story goes that she was having a drink in a Viennese restaurant with Kurt Lewin (known to many of us for his work on change, force field analysis, etc.) when she noticed something remarkable about the waiters. She noticed that they could remember all the orders perfectly as they were going along, but once they'd completed the order, they forgot them totally.

Later she conducted a number of controlled experiments and concluded that people retain information better when the task hasn't been completed than when it has been completed.

In television terms, it's the cliffhanger moment at the end of a series such as *Dallas* that stays with you, making you want to watch the next time to reach some conclusion. Advertisers use these techniques to keep the brandname in your mind while you're watching the advertisement and, hopefully, walking around the supermarket.

I have memories of going to the cinema as a young child on a Saturday morning and seeing the hero in an impossible situation at the end of the reel. I couldn't wait to get back the following week with my 3D glasses (I'm really showing my age now) to see the resolution.

So where is this going? I was considering the training implications. Sometimes on a training course, I would ask people to think about something overnight. I'm never sure if this is a good idea or not. On the one hand, there is the Zeigarnik effect that will keep people interested, but isn't it manipulative?

On the other hand, there's the psychology of completions and incompletions—completions give you energy, incompletions drain your energy. For instance, once you've completed a task and scribbled it off your "to do" list, you get a rush of endorphins that will give you some energy. But having a long list of incomplete tasks will drain your energy, as you will still have these thoughts on your mind. In practical terms, this is why breaking down long tasks into short, manageable tasks is easier. On the other hand, there is the phenomena of completions and incompletions.

However, I digress. Back to Zeigarnik. Would it be better and healthier to draw a line through items on a list at the end of each day? I guess this depends on a variety of factors: how long the incompletion takes to resolve, how meaningful the incompletion is perceived as being (many of the attendees at my courses turn off as soon as they leave the room—whatever I ask them to do), and other things.

But I have one really great idea of how to use this, but I'll save it for another time.

Week 33
Just Turning Up

I was watching a television program the other evening about opera singers. One of the premier singers admitted to having nerves. She said that she often had nights when she wished she would get run over by a bus on the way to the theater to avoid performing that night.

I guess we've all been there. Whether we'd like to admit it or not is another matter, but I've certainly felt like that. Interestingly, for me, this doesn't seem to get any better with age or experience. I learn to control it better and reassure myself that it will be OK as I've done this a hundred times before, but I still get that feeling in the pit of my stomach wondering why I ever did this job in the first place.

Are there any tips or techniques that people could pass on? For me, the main one is talking about it with a colleague. Unfortunately business being business, economics being economics, and training managers coming more from an accountancy background rather than a training background these days, the "luxury" of codelivering seems to be getting less and less, which is a shame really. I have found codelivering far more productive, less stressful, more developmental, and most importantly, better for the attendees.

There are times when only two will do. If it's a long event, an intense event, an event where you need to build up a copresenter's experience, try to explain that to someone holding the budget. There seems to be less and less understanding these days. (I do know how I sound.) It's the same problem facing hospitals, schools, and private companies, as well, I know.

There are lots of things to blame. One major cause of blame would be Anthony Robbins and his like.

"You don't see him copresenting," an admin colleague pointed out recently.

"True. Although I would bet he hasn't got to stand in a queue for 10 minutes waiting to photocopy five sheets for an icebreaker exercise," I replied, a little too jealously. I would guess Anthony has a small army that supports him, and he gets a daily rate approximately equivalent to one calendar year's salary for me. But am I bitter? You know I am. I wonder if he ever gets so worried that he wishes he'd get run over on his way to the theater. I hope so (get worried I mean, not run over).

Week 34
Stereotyping and the Dreaded Night Shift or "We're Special"

When working in large organizations, how often have you heard: "Well that's a good theory, but I'm not sure it would work in our area" or "I like that, but here in (I.M./Sales/H.R.*), it's just not practical given the nature of our work"?

In really large organizations, you can map that onto location as well. Then it's "Well that's a good theory and I'm sure it would work in (Head Office/Regional Offices*), but I really don't think it's for here" or "Not really. It's not a (Welsh/London/New York/Southern*) thing. But I'm sure it would work really well somewhere else."

It is so easy to stereotype groups of people—for example to assume all IM personnel are unhelpful and introverted and have the customer care skills of Genghis Khan. But we know that isn't true. Similarly, it's a common stereotype to assume all Scottish people are mean. We learn through experience that this isn't true, of course. Although I do recall on a recent experience training staff in Glasgow, it proved very stereotypical. A manager from a local office telephoned to ask how much the training course would cost. I explained that it had all been arranged and practically all paid for by the Head Office, but there would be a nominal charge.

"How much?" he asked.

"£20," I said.

"Does that include lunch?"

_____

(*delete as required)

"Yes," I replied.

"And the course," he continued. "When does it start?"

"9:00."

"Finish?"

"5:00."

"And it's £20?" He thought for a while then replied, "It'd better be bloody good."

Building on the stereotype theory, I've delivered a fair amount of training to night shift staff. These people start work at 10:00 p.m. and finish at 6:00 a.m. I've heard from other trainers that they are unappreciated, miserable, and not much fun.

In my experience when I've trained night shift staff, they do think they are the "most special." They do feel they are unappreciated, neglected, and "dumped on." However, I've learned that even though it's a stereotype in most instances, it's true as well. They are often the "out of sight, out of mind" people. They rarely meet senior managers. They are treated as second-class citizens in that the snack bars are rarely open, the vending machines are often empty by the time they start, and they get little chance to meet with HR, IM, or any standard corporate services.

So behind the stereotypes, there may often be some truth or a great deal of truth. I think it's useful to look at these stereotypes and treat this as a useful piece of information—nothing more, nothing less. In terms of the night shift, it certainly helped to understand the frustrations, pressures, and often the negative attitude they have to corporate headquarters. They see me and other trainers as the corporate voice of the organization and often take their frustrations out on trainers, as we are often an easy target, or more accurately, the only target. This used to really frustrate me at the beginning. After listening to the concerns over the years of night shift staff, IM staff, and HR staff, I can appreciate their feelings a little better now.

On the positive side, the night shift staff *are* special. They have a certain sense of "us against them" that bonds them as a team. There is a genuine feeling of looking out for each other, and whatever you do as a trainer, you don't dare single one of them out. Not that you would, but . . .

Week 35
Trainers

So what is it about trainers? They're either dead sensible, chilled individuals who really like a joke and have a sort of "we're all in it together" mentality, or they're finicky, nit-picking, anal-retentive, with no sense of humor, "lets argue for months about whether it's a team exercise or an activity—but on no account is it a game." They're either people who live and let live or people who espouse trust and forgiveness, treat everyone with dignity, and then attack any individual who dares to say anything that could vaguely be interpreted as not politically correct.

Do other professions get this? Do you get groups of doctors who are either laughing at the futility of it all, or are they arguing that even though you saved a life you need to put it in the right code—probably.

OK, I'm done ranting for the moment, but it is a serious point. Working with trainers with no sense of humor is worse than training with an incompetent trainer. At least when you're working with an incompetent trainer you can help them—coach them. With someone with a humor bypass—actually it's not a lack of humor that's the problem but rather a lack of perspective—they give out a sense of smugness when someone makes a mestake (sic).

It's hardly any wonder training has had such a bad reputation in a number of organizations. How often do we come across comments such as:

"Well what would you know about that, living in your ivory tower?"

"Well in the real world . . ."

Training should be about being real—taking risks and looking for support from your colleagues. It mustn't be about looking for things to go wrong then showing off in a patronizing way that you've spotted a mistake. There are a fair amount of trainers out there who don't do anything wrong. Of course they don't, because they don't do anything different—they just use the same safe, boring "developments" they've always used, smile, finish early, and give participants sweets so that they'll give them a decent assessment.

The best trainer I ever worked with often had the worst assessments because he was forever challenging people skillfully, and guess what: they didn't always like it, but they always learned something.

Week 36
Prejudice—Stereotype—
Discrimination

Over the past 10 years or so, I've gotten to the point where I sometimes hardly remember what I've said during a training course as soon as it's finished. This is not the onset of senile dementia, I hope, but rather it is the fact that I've said the same things so often, combined with a sprinkling of the Zeigarnik effect. Sometimes I need to check that I've actually said them, not just thought I've said them. In particular, there are phrases from equal opportunities or diversity courses that I must have said a hundred or more times. The mantra goes something like this:

"We all have prejudices—it's natural. We're born with them or develop them as we grow. These prejudices lead to stereotypes. These stereotypes are shorthand ways of categorizing people. It may happen that the stereotypes come first and form the prejudices. I don't get paid enough to change people's prejudices or stereotypes. What I am paid to do is to deal with the progression of these attitudes when they turn into behavior—discrimination. This is when people act on their prejudices or stereotypes. Discrimination translates as unlawful or unwanted behavior. . . ."

As I said, I often forget the individual words when I get on automatic pilot. However, I have recently become aware of how powerful some of these messages can be. I've noticed that the attitudes of attendees on these courses seem to have changed considerably. Perhaps it's me—perhaps I'm noticing more or just getting more stubborn in my views and values. Perhaps people are changing in the wake of 9/11.

The increased threat of terrorism and their prejudices are becoming more open and they've become more vocal. Or perhaps they've always been like this and I'm just noticing it more. I'm not sure what particular factor or combination of factors applies, but I've certainly noticed a change.

In training events recently, the discussions invariably turn to immigration, and equally invariably, I find that many people have different views than me. This isn't really a problem: I'm used to this on many levels and in many situations, whether it's presenting corporate training or strategic management training. What I've picked up recently though is that the number of people with different views has grown remarkably. Now I wouldn't want to overplay this and pretend that it's every session and every person; however, it has significantly increased.

Anyway, the question is, and there is a question, should we try to change prejudices? Somewhere in the back of my mind there is a little feeling that we should at least try. But then again I guess Stalin, Hitler, and many others felt the same thing. I guess what I mean is that it would be nice if everyone had the same values that I have—but then again we're back to Stalin, Churchill, Thatcher, and Bush. So really it's just a rhetorical question because there is no way we could go down this road.

Week 37
Preparation

Preparation must be the area that causes more grief between trainers and their managers than anything else. It seems to me to be a great indicator of trust, if nothing else.

How much time do you need to prepare? The only answer of course is "It depends." There will be training courses or times in your development when you need a great deal of time and support to get up to speed. Other times, a quick review on the morning train will be sufficient.

The difficulty with this is that it's virtually impossible to say exactly what it depends on. There are training courses that I have run many, many times that I still need to spend a good half day preparing for.

As a training manager, seeing gaps on the schedule must be annoying. "But you're not doing anything on Wednesday." I hear them think as they ask why you can't run three equal opportunity courses back to back.

It's a similar discussion on copresenting. "Why do you need two trainers? There's only one of you talking at a time," I hear. You can launch into a discussion about the course being intense and needing the other trainer to listen and pick up on the group. You talk about the stress of running a three-day course for senior managers on your own. You try to illustrate it with examples of the other trainer picking up an off-the-cuff remark such as "that's not what happened in my area" and discussing this for a while. You try to explain the quality issues. Unfortunately, it's so difficult to quantify. The more we're asked to justify, the more defensive we get and less likely to explain properly. No wonder many training

managers feel it would be easier to get secrets out of the
magic circle than get a trainer to explain what he or she
does between training courses.

These discussions need to take place and need to be as
open as possible. This is difficult. It's tempting to make it
seem like a cartoon situation where the training manager sees
the trainers as trying to get away with doing as little training
as possible, and the trainers see training managers as ogres
with only one thought—bums on seats. It's not really as
simple as that.

For me it's about trust and expertise. If you hired a
qualified plumber to do a job, you wouldn't cross-examine
him about what he's doing, why he's doing it, etc. Yet it does
seem fair game to do this with trainers. One approach that
has worked is to take the training manager with you for
a week. Let her enjoy the delights of trying to find keys
for locked rooms, dealing with projectors that don't work,
moving five tables while attendees are walking in—all those
irritating little things that never happen on their own.

I guess the thinking around preparation is the same:
unless people know what we do, it's natural they will be
suspicious and possibly distrustful. We all know what we
need to do—communicate openly and honestly. It's not
really difficult is it?

Week 38
Coiled Spring

On a recent training course, I used an illustration to get managers thinking about change. It's the idea of their day-to-day workflow being like a coiled spring. The forces acting on the top of the spring are forces driving costs and time down—customers and senior managers wanting products and services cheaper and quicker. The forces acting at the bottom of the spring are quality and quantity being pushed upward—key stakeholders wanting more and of a higher quality. So basically the managers are being asked to balance all these forces, and that is "business as usual." This is quite an act in itself. We discuss some of the issues there—how do you get the balance right? In our job as trainers, I guess we have the same problems: how much time and money do we devote to preparation, research, keeping up to date, training ourselves, etc., and how do we try to increase quality and quantity.

Having worked in the public sector, I realize there is this myth that because the organization isn't driven by profit, the trainers spend a lot of time sauntering around, looking at interesting topics, and going into great depth on all aspects. I wish! The pressures seem to be as intense as any outside organization, and the phrase "best use of public money" seems to crop up quite a lot.

The other aspect of the spring diagram comes when I ask people about changes affecting the organization. I then draw these as arrows trying to knock the spring off balance. There seems to be an overwhelming amount of change wherever you work these days, and it's not long before the flip chart's full of change initiatives, plans, and developments. This seems to be fairly standard in both the public and private sectors.

This was a lot different 15 years ago or so when I was a young computer programmer working for the government. I remember attending a change program—they were rare those days, hence I remember it. During the program, the trainer was telling us about a change initiative that was coming along. It was going to revolutionize the world of us computer programmers. I hurried back to my area, eager to tell everyone. My line manager took me into his office for a quiet word.

"This new program will revolutionize us," I exclaimed. "What shall we do first?"

He looked at me, "Keep your head down."

"But, but . . ."

"Keep your head down. I've been here 30 years, and these programs come and go."

He was absolutely right, that time. However, these days these initiatives don't seem to come and go. They tend to come and stay. A huge problem seems to be the civil servants like my previous manager haven't come and gone either. They're still here and still saying, "Keep your head down."

This is a bit of a problem. . . .

Week 39
The Apex Effect

I've recently come across a phenomenon in alternative medicine known as the Apex Effect, a term coined by Dr. Roger Callahan, pioneer of the energy healing technique known as Thought Field Therapy:

> The apex problem, briefly, is when a client reports a dramatic improvement as the therapy is administered but then fails to give credit to the therapy. The therapy simply appears to be too absurd to be able to effect such dramatic changes. Some clients forget, after successful treatment, that they ever had a problem.

This seems to be an interesting parallel to me in our world. How often have you sat down and worked with someone for hours, even days, and then they've rationalized it away: "Oh our new system solved that," "I've sorted that problem out myself now," "What problem?" In many ways, this is exactly what we're striving for—people to be able to help themselves and not become dependent. In some ways, it's a very mature approach and if people don't recognize the hard work and skill we've put into solving a problem, does it matter? The altruistic answer would be "of course not."

The other answer would be "of course it matters." The reason why it matters can be explained by a number of factors:

1. Being a human as well as a trainer, I like to be appreciated when I achieve something—it makes me feel good.

2. As a business person, how will this help me if people go away saying they've learned nothing?

3. If they go away and acknowledge that they've learned
   something, they will tell others, and I can help even
   more people.

So what should we, as trainers, do? Should we tell
participants in advance that this Apex Effect is a possible
outcome? That would be an option, but it sounds a little
manipulative to me, it may cause a negative reaction, and
they could fight your intervention.

Another suggestion would be to not merely take the
problem away, but to replace it with something. In the case
of healing, this might be replacing pain with a "good feeling."
What could we replace a problem with? I guess we do it
already, don't we? It's called an action plan.

At the end of each course, it seems inevitable that there's
some form of action plan or development log—a piece of
paper that participants have to take away to prove they've
done something and will continue to do something. How
many people carry on with their action plans after a course?
Not many I would guess. How many people get something
out of the course? My guess is a great many. Is this action
plan our way of saying, "Look, I hope you've gotten something from the course, and here's a reminder. We don't
expect you to fill it in, but it has my name on it, so if
you've resolved any problems, I'm the one to thank"?

Is this too harsh? I know there's a lot to be said for
action plans as long as they're relevant, but isn't there
some of this in it?

Couldn't we be more creative than this?

Week 40
It's Only Rock and Roll
but I Like It

Management training is the new rock and roll, or so I've been told. The profile of management gurus has risen a great deal over the past five years or so. Speakers such as Stephen Covey, Kjell Nordstrom, and Jonas Ridderstrale, I'm guessing, charge almost as much per minute as Madonna. They're motivating, amusing, a little evangelical, so I believe. But hey, that's entertainment, isn't it? So is this the new aim of trainers?

Well there is a bit of that I guess. You wouldn't want attendees to start nodding off when you're talking, would you? But then again, you can have too much style without that much substance, can't you? There are some topics we teach that would be extremely difficult to make interesting, aren't there? I would like to see Charles Handy presenting a performance management system half-day overview for job holders and make it riveting.

But I digress: what about us mere mortals? I assume the right thing to say would be "Let's get back to basics. What is the reason for the training? Are the objectives being met? Are the corporate messages being transferred effectively? What is the ROI? What really is the point of training at all?" Fair points . . .

However (and there is a "however"), there's surely more to training than meeting your objectives, passing on the corporate message, explaining the new system. If that's all there is, then that's a great excuse for getting rid of trainers and replacing them with e-learning robots. For me, training is about something more. It's about connecting. The word itself comes from the Latin word *trainore*, meaning connecting to another through words and gestures. Well, OK, I made up that last point, but please . . . we're not lecturers. We're not schoolteachers. We are giving messages, but it's more than that. It's about values. It's about role modeling. If not, then what difference does it make if we're there or not?

Think about training events you've attended as a participant. Which ones do you remember? I guess you don't recall anything about the communication course except the food because the trainer was deathly dull, even though it was exactly what you wanted at the time. I bet the most memorable training event you attended was with that trainer who kept you interested for four days during the potentially dire financial management course.

So entertainment equals good, boring equals bad.
The end.

Well yes, but within limits. You really can have too much of a good thing.

There was a time when there were five trainers on our team, and we knew each other and the course material extremely well. We were definitely trying to "out train" each other. The messages became almost incidental, and we strived to show off and trump each other. On one shameful occasion, a few of us were trying to drop as many song titles into the role plays we were acting. This was interesting and fun—for us. What we forgot was that it's not really about us. I think this is probably the crux of it. Who are we entertaining? If it's for us, then it's showing off. If it's for the attendees to make the event more exciting, memorable, and enjoyable, then surely that's a good thing. If not and people don't get the message completely but have some fun, well it's hardly the end of the world as we know it, is it?

A long time ago, our training team spent two days at a hotel revamping the management development course. After a day and a half of tinkering, we were almost talking ourselves into scrapping the whole program and starting again. Fortunately, we had a wise manager at the time who made us stop and advised us that the course was getting boring for us because we had done it for so long. This didn't mean that it was a boring course. The participants were still really enjoying it, and it was only us who were the problem. We changed a few things, swapped some trainers around, and started really enjoying it again. The course continues to get great reviews (and better evaluations).

Week 41
What Do You Do to Unwind?

It's a strange job we've got as trainers. We're expected to be on our best behavior, acting as role models for eight hours a day. If we're presenting an off-site course, we're expected to carry on that behavior at breakfast, during breaks, over lunch, at dinner, and through the evening. I can't think of many people who have that weight of expectation put on them when they're off duty, apart from priests. Reading the newspapers you'd think it was the reverse—when rock stars or professional athletes are off duty, it seems to be compulsory to smash up a hotel room or get into a fight.

I'm not advocating we resort to that type of behavior, although it would be quite interesting to . . . well perhaps not . . . well not every night. But there must be some release for us.

What I found useful was going out with fellow trainers during long off-site courses to an arcade. There we would happily pay money to shoot course participants. This was a great "shoot 'em up" game where you had computer guns and could line up the bad guys and waste them. Great therapy.

One time myself and a trainer colleague took all the course participants to the Zap Zone. This consisted of a large darkened room with various pieces of equipment to hide behind, and we each had an electronic gun. We split up into two teams and went to war. I'm not sure what the actual objective of the exercise was, but we basically started shooting each other. My colleague ambushed a senior manager who happened to fall over. The rules say something about only shooting someone once when they fall over, but my colleague decided to keep shooting him. The senior manager was most upset and began pleading with my colleague:

"You can't do that. You're only allowed to shoot me once."

Zap—zap—zap.

"Stop it. You really can't cheat like that—you're a *trainer.*"

The tone of incredulity in his voice was as if he was saying "you're a priest."

I guess we've got that power that comes from knowing what's on the next page in the day time. So it's no real surprise that people assume we know what's going to happen next in the evening. It does annoy me at times, though, when course members want you to entertain them in the evening as well as the day.

But that'll be a different rant . . .

Week 42
Presenter's Fears

"Fake it 'till you make it."

Blank looks.

"Pretend you can do something, and keep doing it until you wake up one morning and find you really can. Pretend you're really confident about presenting. Visualize someone who does it well. Copy them. Really. Trust me. Try it. It works."

They trust me. They try it. It works—for some of them.

Presentations are the most feared part of most managers' lives. I've read that most managers would prefer the stress caused by moving house than giving a 10-minute presentation. To some extent I get it. It can be intimidating to stand up in front of a room full of people and talk. A lot of the blame must go to "presentation skills courses." Yes, it's nice to be able to project your voice to the back of the room. It's great to have exciting slides. It's superb if you can manage the correct eye contact with your audience. Unfortunately, within a few minutes of the start of the presentation, most of the audience has taken this for granted. The message is far more important. Get that right in your own head, and you're winning.

"What's the worst that can happen?" I ask.

The replies tend to fall into two categories: physical and mental. On the physical side, there's the projector failing or no projector, no flip-chart paper, no pens, not enough chairs, too many chairs, etc. Go through your list one by one and ask yourself "what could I do if that happened?" and plan for it. Think of everything that could go wrong and plan an alternative. If something you haven't thought of goes wrong, as is inevitable, well—how important is it? How many other aspects of your life have gone 100 percent to plan all the time, every time? Exactly.

The good thing is that people don't judge us on the mistakes we make, but on our speed of recovery from those mistakes. Think of the best customer care you've received. Nine out of ten times people recall a situation that went wrong. It went wrong, but the service they received to put it right made them remember it and recommend the company to their friends years after.

The other category of things that can go wrong concerns the mental side. Preparation is the key, and it should start right from the moment it's decided you're the one for the presentation. It doesn't get easier the longer you ignore it. You know this, so start finding out about the presentation's objectives as soon as possible—on the day you are in charge.

If you know exactly what you want to convey, the best way to get that across is by interacting from the start. Find out what the audience knows and doesn't know. Find out why they're there. Find out their particular interests. It may well be more nerve-racking than hiding behind a script, but it is so much more rewarding. But this can only happen if you've got your head straight first. To do this, you need to ask questions and get them to ask you questions.

How presenters deal with questions by the audience is a tremendous indication of where they are in terms of confidence. If the first line in a presentation is "I'll take questions at the end," then the odds are the trainer

a) is petrified;

b) has no idea what he or she is talking about; or

c) has hours' worth of material and will never reach the end.

Week 43
Unfair Competition in the Workplace or How Venusians Get a Job on Mars

I am reluctant to write about one particular issue for trainers, HR people—this issue concerns differences between men and women. I have noticed that in most publications, deal with HR issues one step away from the politically correct line and the writer gets savaged. This fear of saying the wrong thing is becoming a real problem in training rooms. It's not that we (trainers) deliberately try to discriminate or offend, but mistakes happen. I've been castigated on a few occasions for not including a woman (or man) when I've selected training groups for break-out work. There was a time long, long ago when I was mortified and felt like such a sexist pig for failing to have the right mix. Luckily I've become far more comfortable admitting mistakes—perhaps due to the fact that I've had more practice.

So what is the difference between men and women? Good question. The difference I'm referring to concerns interviewing and competition in the workplace. Interview training is something I've done a fair amount of, and it never occurred to me that there could be potential problems for women ("Why would you—being a man?" I often hear).

There is always competition in the workplace. If people acknowledge this, then it is overt competition and often healthy. If they fail to acknowledge this, then it is covert competition and invariably destructive. Individuals will compete to be the most popular, the least popular, the most productive, the least productive. . . .

A psychologically interesting example of a potential problem occurred recently when a senior management role was advertised with a salary of £55,000 per year. There were no women applicants. However, when the same post was readvertised with a salary of £35,000 per year, the advertisers were overwhelmed with applications from women.

On a more day-to-day level, I've started thinking about interviewing. There are some differences between men and women. (My disclaimer here: I know this doesn't apply to everyone and people shouldn't make assumptions, etc., etc. I'm not saying it's a good or bad thing—it's just a thing.) Men tend to be more aggressive, and in a workplace situation, this can often show itself as taking more risks than women. This has been established through a number of recent studies. Women tend to choose high probability, low payoff strategies. Men will often rush to a high-risk solution and take a chance in a "do or die" gesture. The implications of this behavior in assessments may well suggest to interviewers (who are more often than not, male) that the female lacks confidence or competence.

In a recent study, Fisher and Cox argue that this could well be the underlying reason women, on average, take longer to respond to questions. This can often indicate to interviewers a degree of indecisiveness. In fact, women may well need to weigh all the options. This will be compounded by the fact that women are generally less likely to take guesses than men. Under pressure, perhaps at an interview or in an assessment, men would be more inclined to take a stab at an answer. Women would tend to want to consider the situation and assess the risks. In a real work environment, one would suppose that these virtues of balance and control would be ideal. In the artificial assessment situation, however, this failure to respond quickly is often taken as an indicator of lack of confidence.

There are a lot more data behind this and numerous other factors. I feel it is, at the least, interesting and, at worst, possibly discriminatory. It's an area we, certainly I, have never considered before when training interviewers or interviewees. Maybe I should.

Week 44
Away Days,
Team-Building Events, etc.

If you've been asked to facilitate an away day, a strategic day, a visioning day, a team-building day, a scenario planning event, or anything else that involves taking a group of people away from the workplace, you need to spend a fair amount of time talking beforehand.

First you need to make sure you talk to the right person. Don't talk to the personal assistant, the organizer, the training manager, or anyone but the client. Then when you negotiate, discuss, or just agree to do something, you need to go through a strict process. It may seem hard and time consuming, but trust me, when you get into the habit, it will save you so much time and anxiety that you'll wonder how you survived before.

A great amount of time and effort is expended because people don't have a useful discussion—an effective wanted and needed conversation. This is the key to any form of negotiation. Both parties need to establish exactly what's required, by when, by whom, and where the responsibilities lie.

Truly effective negotiators learn to handle this part of the conversation extremely effectively. They communicate skillfully by talking, listening, and staying in the conversation until they are totally sure of the goal. This can be difficult. How often have you been introduced to someone and not caught their name? Do you ask them to repeat it? How often? The really expert communicator will ask for as many times as it takes. We all know the problems if we don't do this, don't we? We spend the rest of the evening avoiding the person or

feeling embarrassed when we talk to him or her. This can go
on for weeks. I've known people who didn't catch someone's
name on the first day at the office, and as the weeks went by,
became too embarrassed to ever ask them.

So back to the wanted and needed conversation: you
need to establish what the other person truly needs, not
just wants. For instance, in my former role as a consultant,
I frequently met managers who wanted a team-building day.

"That's what I want and that's what I need," they
would claim.

There needed to be a great deal of skillful communication
to tease this out. Starting with lots of open questions:

- "Why do you feel you need this?"

- "What are the problems now?"

- "What do you want this team-building day to achieve?"

- "How will you know if this event was successful?"

- "How will you be able to demonstrate this?"

Ask questions and listen to the replies. Invariably, what
the person needs doesn't match with what they think they
want initially. Team-building days tend to occur when there
are a few members of staff disrupting the team, or the team
members aren't clear about their roles, or there's no direction
from the leader, etc. You need to be as specific as possible
about the problem and ensure the other is clear about the
problem and what he or she wants and needs. Now you've
got something tangible to work with.

The key to this is asking effective questions. And how
do you ask effective questions, you ask? You ask effective
questions when you listen effectively. You listen to the person. You listen to what they say, what they don't say, how
they say it. Listen to that little voice inside you. If something

doesn't feel right, it usually isn't. Do it now rather than in a few weeks' time in front of 20 senior managers on a strategic day.

If you aren't sure, then ask. This doesn't need to be a big thing. Just tell the truth: "Well you say there are no problems between any of the staff, but I have a feeling there may be. Can you tell me a bit more about this?" Stay in that conversation until you have no doubts at all and are completely sure what's expected. This may seem incredibly strange to begin with, but trust me, it will save you so much stress in the long term.

The next part of the discussion is about your willingness and ability to meet that request—a willing and able conversation. You need to honestly ask yourself whether you are willing and able to meet the request. Do you have the necessary skills, knowledge, and attributes to make it work? If you don't, then say so and try to work out a way to still help—suggest others, look at different approaches, but again stay in the conversation. Don't stop and walk away before you're absolutely 100 percent sure you know what's expected of you. You know from experience that this won't work, don't you? The "problem-solving fairy" doesn't miraculously appear and sort things out when you ignore them. They just stay there and grow and grow.

So deal with these problems as they arise. Stay there until you're happy and the other person is happy. This all seems so clear and sensible, I know, but it can be difficult. The good thing though is that it does get easier. The more you do it, the easier it gets.

Once this has been resolved, the event should be relatively straightforward—well except for those 101 things that can go wrong during any training event. There are a few tips for the day, and they involve preparation and speed of recovery.

Number one tip: Don't believe anyone. Check everything. Don't let anyone book anything for you. Don't believe anyone when they say, "Oh yes, that won't be a problem." Do everything yourself. This is based on many bad experiences of projectors not being there, chairs not being there, doors being locked, the training room being next to the elevator, coffee being served late. OK, perhaps this isn't the most practical advice and there may be no option but to delegate. If you absolutely have to, then delegate to someone who has been there and knows what it feels like to stand in front of 200 people with no idea how the new-fangled projector works.

The other factor has to do with "speed of recovery." You know things will go wrong. You need to accept that and concentrate on fixing them rather than getting upset about them. The time for investigation can come later. Things will go wrong, and as the facilitator, you're expected to fix it. So fix it and move on. I have found that people are fairly forgiving of mistakes. Things happen. People tend to judge you on how you handle them. The best suggestion I have is to establish a name and number of someone at the hotel or training venue who can help and you can trust. Then when something happens, use them and sort it out, as blamelessly, seamlessly, and professionally as possible.

One final point to do with actions arising from the event: beware of social loafing. It's tempting as it gets near the end of the day to let things slip. Now is the time to concentrate for that final effort. You should have a list of actions that you've collected throughout the day. As you come to review the actions, ensure that someone takes responsibility for them, knows exactly what they should do, and has a date to report on it. Beware of actions that are signed up to "B3 Section" or "all managers" or similar groups. These are doomed.

Costas Markides refers to this phenomenon as social loafing and has some poignant examples to illustrate this. He tells the story of Kitty Genovese and her brutal murder on March 14th, 1964, in New York.

For more than half an hour, 38 respectable, law-abiding citizens in Queens watched a killer stalk and stab a woman in three separate attacks in Kew Gardens. Twice their chatter and the sudden glow of their bedroom lights interrupted him and frightened him off. Each time he returned, sought her out, and stabbed her again. Not one person telephoned the police during the assault. One witness called after the woman was dead.

This is an extreme example of social loafing, but similar things happen when groups are asked to take action. There is a thought that someone else will do it. Be wary of making that assumption.

Week 45
There Are Options—
But Not That Many

It's been a typical middle management strategic day. It's been difficult and frustrating, and I'm wondering why I bother. I understand people's frustrations—I really do—but do we have to go through them every time? Of course we do—it's called being human.

It started as usual with a "poor us" session—"We're special," "My manager doesn't understand me," "In the private/public sector things are different. . . ." Inevitably, it came around to the question of blame. Guess whose fault it was. Yes—it was *them* (finger pointing upward). It always seems to be *them*.

I pointed out that I asked the same question in a session I ran with their managers. Their managers had also identified the culprits as *them* (finger pointing upward). I also explained that this had happened a month ago at a meeting I held with their staff. They identified the culprits as *them* (finger pointing upward).

(I wonder how far up this pointing would go. Perhaps it only stopped when you reached God or some divine being that couldn't pass the buck any higher.) It's not a surprise—although there were some surprised faces in the room. So we talked a little more calmly. I picked this up from a trainer who used to tell people that if there was one finger pointing out at people, there had to be four pointing at themselves.

I guess there are basically only four options for dealing with the frustrations and barriers in the workplace. You can

- **change yourself.** We talked a fair amount about this. There is the analogy of a jigsaw. You are a piece of a jigsaw puzzle. Whenever you attend a training course, have an insight, or even do something or think something differently, then you change. When you go back to the workplace, you simply don't fit. Many people spend some time trying to fit, but eventually return to their previous shape and fit in again. Some people may fight and fight for a long time—then eventually they give up. I see them wandering the corridors like zombies. I hear them at meetings—or rather, I don't hear them at meetings (apart from the rhythmic nodding of their heads). It's a life—but it's not a life.

- **leave the situation.** This is, for some people, not even an option they can consider. It is as ridiculous to them as flying to the moon. "Leave? But I can't. I've been here for x years—I wouldn't survive in the outside world," said one 52-year-old, £50,000-a-year, senior statistician. This was true—he wouldn't.

- **negotiate for change.** This seemed to be the best option, so we had a good look at this. As a jigsaw piece, how do you subtly change the other pieces around you to allow you to fit in again? We looked at the problems, the options, the strategies, the barriers, and the skills. The biggest motivator, as always, seems to be themselves—the talking, the sharing of problems, the tiny successes.

After a good few hours, it was time to leave and, on the whole, it was positive. Before they left, however, they asked about the fourth option.

This is an option a number of their colleagues seemed to be embracing wholeheartedly:

- **Stay and be miserable.**

Week 46
Players and Managers

It's a well-established fact (probably) that great players never make great managers.

Recently sparked off by several great footballers retiring and going into management, I've been thinking about footballers/managers. My contention is that you rarely get an outstanding footballer becoming an outstanding manager.

For instance, if you consider the 1966 England World Cup winning team, only one player, Jack Charlton, has had any success as a manager. All of today's top Premiership managers—Jose Murinho, Alex Ferguson, Arsène Wenger, Rafael Benitez—were all "journeymen" professionals, as indeed was the manager of this year's Italian World Cup winning team, Marcello Lippi.

I recognize that my examples are predominantly European and football based, but I challenge you to apply this to your particular sport/country/city and see if it works.

Applying this logic to our situation, it would mean that we would be better off managed by "journeymen" trainers rather than the excellent superb trainers. Logically, this seems absolutely true. There are a whole different set of skills to being a trainer and managing trainers. It's obviously a similar case in football or any other sport. Tiger Woods's coaches aren't Jack Nicklaus and Arnold Palmer; they are Hank Haney and Butch Harmon, two competent golf professionals who never won majors. What they do have is a great understanding of the techniques and psychology of golf. When you equate skill in one role to skill in another role, it can be a disaster. In England, think Paul Gascoigne; other countries can supply their own examples.

In my experience, there seems to be two approaches to take when appointing training managers: you get an excellent trainer and promote him or her to manage trainers—a strange approach equivalent to promoting an excellent hospital porter to becoming a surgeon—or you move a manager into the training area because he or she is an effective manager in another area. Again I see this fraught with dangers. If you look at Murinho, Wenger, and the rest, they have all played the game at a competitive level. In purely prosaic terms, I would like to be managed by someone who knows what it's like to have to train when the overhead projector breaks down or when three-quarters of the participants don't want to be there.

For me, this works out in purely practical terms—I want a manager who will call me and check how I did after running a new course for the first time. I want a manager who will appreciate that after eight hours of a stressful course, it's OK to get a taxi rather than cross London via the underground in order to save £8 of the training budget.

I see this as a problem that most organizations fail to address. The better ones will have a stab at it and make a token gesture that invariably means the trainers are managed by someone from a personnel background. To senior managers, the words *HR, training, personnel, development,* and *learning* are all synonyms. But that's a rant for another day.

Week 47
The Benefits of Telling the Truth

A long time ago, I was running my very first consultancy session. It was particularly stressful because I was training a group of economists in the delights of team building over two days. At that time, I had an over-inflated view of economists. I used to put them on a pedestal. I was never particularly good with math and was in awe of anyone who was. I did think economists were incredibly clever, knew everything, and basically had brains the size of planets.

The session was the first in the program. At first it seemed that things were going well. Then one of the economists, the most senior economist, asked a question. This was fine. I'd been asked questions before, but there was something about the way he asked that didn't feel right. Bear in mind my feeling toward economists, and this person was the top economist. This person had worked with members of Parliament and was the one who was wheeled out at press conferences. He had the reputation of computing the most difficult calculations in his head.

Anyway, I answered his question and carried on with the session. Again, the senior economist stopped the session to ask a question. Now there are at least two things going on in my mind at this point. In one half there's the logical, rational part thinking, "perhaps I'd better slow down, or explain things more carefully—it's obvious that this guy needs more time." However the other part of my brain was screaming, "Help! What an idiot I am. I hate this job. Why am I so useless?"

By the time the session was over, I was practically a
nervous wreck. There were more questions, and I could
feel myself turning toward the others in the group,
almost shunning this individual.

The end of the day couldn't come quick enough. Dinner
with everyone was a tense time, and all I wanted to do was
go to bed and forget it. However, as I sat in the hotel room,
I began thinking about the day. I decided that I had to do
the right thing. I'd been talking about honesty, disclosure,
and Johari window, so I decided if I was to maintain any
credibility, I had to put the theory into action.

Slightly nervously, I went down to the bar and saw
three or four of the group chatting away. I joined them
and took a deep breath and told them I wasn't sure that
the senior statistician had gotten anything out of it. I started
explaining how I felt and how intimidated I was and could
see the others laughing.

"Well I don't think it's very funny," I said.

"No, no. We're not laughing at you," one of them said.
"We're laughing at the economist."

"Why's that?"

"Well he has the reputation for being incredibly
sharp, and he can answer questions in his head, but
they're never right."

"Really?"

"Never right. You shouldn't trust anything he says. He's
good at the big picture but hopeless at the details, which is
why he asks lots of questions. It takes him a long time to
really understand things."

I'll leave you to work out the moral of the story, but it
has helped me a great deal over the years.

There is a follow-up to this: a year ago I was at Heathrow
Airport and met the economist. We had had many laughs

about the situation over the years, but, there was still something in the back of my mind about the situation. Anyway, he was going to the Ukraine as I was. He was staying at the same hotel, and we arranged to meet later that evening. Now this was my tenth trip to the Ukraine, and I knew where things were. I knew the country a little. I knew the hotel. The economist had never been before.

"Great," I thought, uncharitably, "I'm in charge now."

Later that evening, we met in a restaurant, and the statistician asked if I wanted a beer. I accepted and he called a waiter over and ordered two beers in Ukrainian. Suddenly I was back in the classroom in England. I had those same feelings of intimidation and self-doubt creeping back.

The waiter arrived with two bottles of water, not beer. As always, the economist had picked up a phrase and used it. He said it confidently, but it was totally wrong.

How we laughed.

Week 48
The Dangers of
Large Organizations

The opening gambit of a culture change program;

> The CEO of an organization asks all department
> heads to send any spare money or resources back
> to corporate headquarters to fund one particular
> vital project.
>
> Two weeks later, the head of IM has a meeting with
> a divisional director on an operations team.
>
> "That looks like a really sensible project. Maybe we
> can do something with it next quarter."
>
> "Why not now?" inquires the divisional director.
>
> "Well you heard that all the spare resources have
> gone back to corporate headquarters. I won't have
> any money until the next quarter."
>
> "Don't worry about the money. I have some
> tucked away."

Now I'm sure something similar wouldn't happen
to you. Well I'm fairly sure if you work in an
organization of less than 150 people. This seems
to be a sort of magic number for organizations.
As an organization grows, it seems that communication problems and hidden agendas emerge far
more obviously when there are 150 employees
(give or take 10).

It seems that once an organization grows and
splits into various silos, the problems multiply

dramatically. A real tension develops for managers between the aims of the organization as a whole and running their own part of the business.

I worked in a large public company where one business area recruited 100 staff for a particular project that for a variety of reasons was postponed for six months. These extra staff were contracted for a year and were just sitting around doing next to nothing.

The head of the area announced to the rest of the organization, "Sorry—screwed up. I have 100 spare staff. Who would like them?"

The conversations with various managers went something like this:

"How much would these staff cost me?"

"Nothing. We've arranged to pay them from my budget, so they wouldn't cost you a penny."

"Who will write their performance evaluations?"

"I'm sure we can work that out when the time comes."

"Where will they sit? Who will they report to?"

"Forget it. Seems more trouble than it's worth."

This silo mentality is a huge obstacle in organizations. There seems to be a real problem breaking down the walls. The more established the organization, it seems the tougher the walls. It gets to the stage where each silo is almost a self-contained unit. While there are real benefits here (operating as a small business, good communications within the area, sense of pride in the silo "team"), there are huge disadvantages as highlighted. The problems of communication across areas and sharing resources and people seem to outweigh the advantages. It becomes rare to loan people out or move people. Budgets are guarded. Corporate headquarters becomes the enemy. For instance, toward the end of the financial year, large organizations tend to look at budgets for specific areas. I've worked with departments that would have a spending frenzy in March. When asked why they were going crazy buying far more pencils, paper clips, and pens than they could ever use, it was explained that if they didn't spend their allocated budget, then it would be cut next year.

When I asked why they didn't explain this to the Finance area, I was given the "you don't know how it works around here" look.

It seems that the values at the center don't apply to the departments. There's the "they're not our values" mentality. This isn't necessarily just about a silo mentality. There is a problem with values. They sound good. No one would argue with them. But how far would people actually go to uphold them? In recent years, there have been a number of organizations in which the values seem to have been ignored by everyone—Enron, Parmalat, Shell, for instance—and I guess some of this has to do with a "silo mentality."

Split into three groups and discuss for about three days.

Week 49
History of Feedback

For many, many years, well before I started in training, feedback was taught as a very methodical, very black-and-white process. The feedback was meant to be observable, measurable, objective, and had a very clear, easy-to-follow three-part process:

Part 1: Observed, specific, nonexaggerated description of behavior

Part 2: The effect it had on me/my team/the organization

Part 3: What I'd like you to do about it

The feedback had slight variations, but an example went somewhere along the following lines:

> "When I worked with you yesterday, you left me to do all the cleaning up at the end of the day. This took me half an hour and I'd like you not to do it again."

This was the generally accepted method. Later there was an additional element where you told the other how you felt about it:

> "When I worked with you yesterday, you again left me to do all the cleaning up. This again took half an hour, and I'm disappointed with you."

It seemed like a Catholic approach as it often had the effect of making people change their behavior by guilt.

There was a great deal of emphasis on making the feelings primary feelings of disappointment, hurt, fear, concern, etc., rather than the secondary feelings of anger. The example I used to give was of me having a rare evening out with a colleague. Before I'd leave to go out, I would casually announce, "I won't be late." Unfortunately, I'm having a great time and don't even think about the time until it's 2:00 in the morning. Now I ask participants to consider the feelings of my cartoon wife. What is she feeling as the hours go on? Then it happens: she hears my knock at the front door (I've lost my key), and the first reaction, the primary feeling, is relief. This is rapidly followed by a rush of secondary feelings—anger being at the top of the list.

This worked. It especially worked for people who felt very uncomfortable giving feedback. People who worked in areas where this wasn't the norm liked it especially. No doubt some IT programmers built little subroutines to code this in: description = _____, effect = _____, desired output = _____, primary feeling = _____.

There were, however, a number of problems with this approach. For instance, it didn't address what would happen if the other person did nothing about it. It didn't consider the other person's feelings at all. It was very much about the effect on you. Also, it was so structured it was impossible to give anyone feedback you hadn't actually observed firsthand.

Then thinking moved on a little. Another avenue looked at why people don't like to give feedback. This was interesting. I was involved in many difficult training sessions. I would ask people to write some examples of feedback they hadn't delivered and why they hadn't delivered them. The reasons were all pretty much the same: no time, wasn't worth it, didn't feel it would make any difference, they were a higher/lower priority to me, etc.

My contention was that all these defenses were just excuses for the real reason: they were too arrogant to tell the other person. This tended to raise the temperature. My explanation went like this: "Would you have liked to know about the criticism if it had been the other way around?" I threw in some of their examples: "If you'd kept them waiting for 20 minutes. If you'd given them poor service." Invariably they answered with a resounding yes. I continued. "So if you would like to know, why wouldn't they? Are you saying, at some level, that you're better than them? You could handle the criticism, but they couldn't?" This was usually an interesting moment.

There is a lot of truth here. There's also a fair amount of blame on my part; I guess I antagonized people. Over time, I've managed to handle this better. The following illustration helped:

> I worked with a consultant who told the story of being in his final year of University and taking final exams. During this time, his grandmother died. His parents didn't want to upset him and didn't tell him about this and her subsequent funeral until after his exams. When they did tell him, he went ballistic.

His parents were trying to do the right thing, obviously, but it wasn't. This lead to the ethos of giving feedback with love and without compromise. You focus on your intention for giving feedback. If you want to give feedback to show off, score points, or demonstrate your cleverness, then don't do it. You give feedback purely with the intention of helping the other. You give feedback because you love them, not because you hate them. We have no problem giving our friends and family harsh feedback however unskillfully: *"You're not going out dressed like that are you?" "Yes, actually—your bum does look big in that."* We do it because we love them and want them to change—sorry. The words often don't matter—it's the intention that's all important.

In recent times, feedback did start to consider the feelings of the other person. It's not enough to have a pure intention;

you need to consider the effect as well. My intention could be to make you become the best leader on the planet. However, if you get so annoyed with my inane criticisms that you leave the company after three days, that's not really going to help anyone, is it? So consider both aspects: intention and effect.

The most recent aspect has been on the words and the specifics. In psychological terms, there are people who prefer dealing with reality, structure, and order. There are others who prefer the intuitive, gut-reaction approach. The realists have done well out of feedback so far. It has had to be real, observable, and measurable. Now the emphasis is on the other aspect as well. If you can't pinpoint an incident, it doesn't mean that you've now got to ignore your feelings. For instance, it's useful on many management courses to build in an exercise for people to give each other feedback on how they have come across to them during the few days of the course. This gives people a useful idea of how others see them. It helps if there's a structured process and often a list of suggested questions for the realists: "What were your first impressions of x and how have they changed throughout the five days?" for instance. It's also useful to emphasize that the feedback doesn't have to be observable: it can be intuitive: "I can't explain why, but during the first exercise, I had a sense that you were getting frustrated." This can be really useful. It doesn't mean that the observer is factually accurate (the other may have been feeling tired or thinking about something else), but it does allow them to discuss feelings and how they may come across to others. This in itself is useful feedback.

So feedback changes and will no doubt continue to change. My favorite feedback was from a former manager when I asked him how I was performing.

"You're still here," came the reply.

Week 50
Diversity—
Tips for Dealing with People

Diversity training can be difficult. Training new managers to manage people with disabilities can be very difficult. The approach I've adapted is basically not to do anything different. This is based on the belief that people with disabilities want to be managed the same as all of us. This doesn't mean treating everyone the same. People aren't the same. Everyone is different. People have different talents, and it's for managers to bring those talents out. This doesn't mean you have to ignore someone's disability—deal with it. The easiest way of doing this is by talking about it. This raises another problem in managers' minds: How do you get the right balance between being intrusive and appearing uncaring?

My advice is to trust your feelings. If you feel there is a problem, you should address it. There will be no need to pry or ask personal questions. Have an adult conversation about your concerns and listen to the reply. Don't ignore the problem and hope it will go away. You know that never happens.

If possible, attend a training program. Hopefully this should achieve a few things for you: first it should help reinforce all the things you are already doing well, and second it should help raise your awareness of issues.

Some of the lessons I learned from a course I attended 10 years ago have still stuck with me. One exercise was particularly traumatic for a number of us taking the course. The instructors asked us to choose our disability. This was extremely hard. People were getting very upset imagining this. Eventually we had all chosen—some were blind, deaf, etc. Then they introduced the second part of the exercise.

"Now, what can't you do?" we were asked.

Initially there was a great deal of debate about all the things we couldn't do if we were in a wheelchair, visually impaired, etc., but after a while, we started to realize that there weren't a great many barriers for us. Or at least if there were barriers, there were ways around them. Most of these obstacles existed in our heads. OK, so being blind I was unlikely to win the 100-meter Olympic title. But as a trainer pushing 40 and not being particularly fit would tend to suggest that anyway.

The facilitator gave us an eye-opening example of the stereotyping that wheelchair users come across. One day he was sitting in his wheelchair outside Marks and Spencer waiting for his wife and drinking a can of coke. A middle-aged woman walked past, looked at him, opened her purse, took out a pound coin, and dropped it in his can. "There," she smiled and walked off.

The tip is to address the issue and talk about it. For example, if a member of your staff is in a wheelchair and has problems opening a heavy door, say, "Excuse me, I can see that you're in a wheelchair struggling to open that heavy door. Do you need some help?"

It's not difficult, is it?

Week 51
Ho! Ho! Ho! And All That

Ah, the holiday season. It's a time for taking stock and slowing down. It's a time to start thinking about your career—reliving those ups and downs of the past year and wondering if you've got the energy to carry on in this strange profession.

It's a time for thinking. Training courses in late December are rarer than an original idea in a "24" series. It's gift-giving time, and unluckily (or luckily), there's no "easy" gift for a management consultant/trainer/developer/facilitator/or whatever we're called these days.

Every other corner of every other store seems to have a dedicated industry selling those things at this time of year (or rather selling it to people who think this is what people want). Do you think any avid angler wants the PS2 game of Fisherman's Challenge? Or taxi drivers will be queuing up (sorry) to own Taxi Driver on Xbox?

There may well be a need out there for a virtual management trainer. I can see it now: it's a mixture of a "shoot 'em up" game and Championship Manager. You get to skillfully plan all the tactics, but if things start going wrong. . . .

Maybe there are a number of levels to this. You start off on level one running a nice, easy straightforward induction course. The attendees are all new—it's their first real job apart from their three weeks washing dishes in a restaurant, and they are excited, interested, and totally uncynical.

By the time you get to level six, you're running strategic away days for a group of smart, interested, cynical, critical, stressed, highly intelligent 50 something executives who have seen it all, done it all, and . . . this could be when that laser gun comes in useful.

Or perhaps there's a market for "Trainergotchi."™
Looking at the instructions, it sounds pretty much like
every trainer I've known:

Development of the Creature

Early stage:

It is very timid and does not move around much. It
will make frequent demands for your attention.

Rebellious stage:

It will often thrash about wildly at this stage. It also
learns to communicate.

Adolescent stage:

It becomes able to play alone, take baths of its own
accord, etc.

All it needs is some care and attention (feedback
and praise).

When your creature starts crying or calling out to
you, select a Care icon and give it the care it needs.
If you don't take appropriate action while the sign
is flashing, your creature could develop the habit
of pestering you, or its development could become
stunted. The care you give it will affect its future
development and determine its adult character.

Maybe it's not for me. Sounds like the ideal gift for my
manager though.

Week 52
Last Week

On the week that one of my colleagues and favorite trainers moves on, I started thinking about "leaving dos" and trainers' farewell parties in particular. They have tended to be pretty raucous affairs, involving copious amounts of alcohol, stories of training events past, and a general air of nostalgia.

I guess it's the mutual understanding of the stress we are often under that tends to make trainers a breed apart (although I dare say other professions would pretend they were special as well).

On one such occasion, a few of us, fairly late in the evening, started thinking about winning the lottery, as you do, and what our final fantasy training event would be (sad, I know, but we had had a few beers). Everyone had one or two favorite people they would invite. The best was a trainer who had delivered a pretty gruelling, but crucial two-day event to senior managers explaining the financial plight the organization was under. At the end, she felt most of the managers had gotten it. As she was tidying up at the end of the second day, the CEO walked toward her. "Well, he's finally going to thank me for something," she thought, having worked for this particular CEO for many years with only a cursory grunt as recognition.

"Thanks for that," said the CEO. "Do you want some feedback?"

"Of course."

"I found it turgid."

We could all identify three or four characters that started every sentence with "Ah, but in the real world. . . ."

I seem to recall senior managers who kept getting called away for "urgent meetings" that turned out to coincide with pub opening hours. We fantasized about getting them all together in one room, locking the door, and delivering the "domestics":

"This is my last week of training. Yes, I'll miss it. It is my last week of sitting crammed in a second-class train carriage from Liverpool to London, working out how much money I can spend of my £21 per-night on beer if I've got to buy two meals in London (or more likely go to the nearest Sainsbury's supermarket for a trainer's veggie special—three packets of crisps, a cheese pasty, four bread rolls, 10 economy processed cheese slices, and a copy of the *London Evening Standard* to see what's on TV). Then I'll get back to my tiny, tiny hotel room with barely enough space for a bed and shower and nothing to watch except CNN or Eurosport. Then the remote control won't work, but I know that you have to take the batteries out, warm them in your hand, then replace them.

"I'll miss talking to a bunch of people who don't want to be here—where the only question you'll listen intently to is 'what time do we finish?' and will give me top marks if I give you an hour for lunch and let you go home half an hour early. God I'll miss this. This week will be special though. This week is the week I run this course properly—you will have critical feedback like it's going out of fashion. I've got a four-ring binder on each of you and we're going to work through it at my pace. The doors are locked. It's just me and you.

"Any questions?"

References

Adams, Hayes, & Hopson (1976). *Transition: understanding and managing change.* London: Martin Robertson.

Blanton, B. (2000). *Practicing radical honesty.* Sparrowhawk Publications.

Brehm, J. W. (1966). *A theory of psychological reactance.* Academic Press.

Deutschman, A. (May 2005). Change or die. *Fast Company.*

Fisher, M., & Cox, A. (2006). Gender and programming contests: mitigating exclusionary practices. *Informatics in Education.*

Gladwell, M. (2005). *Blink: the power of thinking without thinking.* Little, Brown and Company.

About the Author

Byron Kalies has been a management trainer for the past 13 years. He has worked for a range of organizations in a range of (largely nonexotic) countries: Poland, Lesotho, Hungary, and Ukraine. For the past 5 years or so, he has become a management writer appearing in a wide range of international publications including *Across the Board* (United States), *The Training Report* (Canada), *Guardian* (U.K.), *Sydney Morning Herald* (Australia), *Business Day* (South Africa), and *Business Plus* (Ireland).